If I Knew It Was
Going to Be This
Much Fun, I Would Have
Become a
Grandparent First

⌘

ALSO BY Willard Scott AND FRIENDS

The Older the Fiddle, the Better the Tune

If I Knew It Was Going to Be This Much Fun, I Would Have Become a Grandparent First

Willard Scott

AND FRIENDS

New York

Library of Congress Cataloging-in-Publication Data

Scott, Willard.
    If I knew it was going to be this much fun, I would have
  become a grandparent first / Willard Scott.
      p. cm.
    ISBN 1-4013-0063-4
    1. Grandparenting. 2. Grandparent and child. I. Title.

HQ759.9.S37 2004
306.874'5—dc22

                                2003067593

Hyperion books are available for special promotions and premi-
ums. For details contact Michael Rentas, Manager, Inventory and
Premium Sales, Hyperion, 77 West 66th Street, 11th floor,
New York, New York 10023-6298, or call 212-456-0133.

FIRST EDITION

10 9 8 7 6 5 4 3 2 1

To my grandchildren,
Sallie Marie and John Swiatek.
And to my adopted grandson,
Al Roker.

Acknowledgments

This collection could not have come together without the help of my friends at Bill Adler Books, Inc. Bill Adler, Jan Crozier, and Mary Nettleton: We did it again! I would also like to thank Bill Adler, Jr., Peggy Robin, Julia Beizer, Ami Dodson, and Jeanne Welsh of Adler & Robin Books, Inc., whose research and editing skills guided this book from infancy to ripe old age. Additional thanks to Kiera Hepford at Hyperion, who has simply been a joy to work with.

Thank you to all of the contributors for taking the time to share your heartwarming stories. Special thanks to Billie Brown Simmons for contributing such a touching family keepsake. I would also like to thank DJ McQuade of National Grandparents Day Council, Jan Stover, and Sandy Brokaw for their efforts behind the scenes.

Finally, greatest thanks to the grandchildren of the world. You continue to bring us grandparents joy, each and every day.

If I Knew It Was
Going to Be This
Much Fun, I Would Have
Become a
Grandparent First

Introduction

Why do we love our grandparents so much? Part of the reason I think has to do with the tremendous natural affection and affinity that kids have for older people, whether they are their actual grandparents or not. I know that when I was a kid in Sunday school I used to look forward to the end of church because there was a lady, Mrs. Earl Brinkle, who was probably about seventy-five years old and always wore a little nine-dollar JCPenney dress. I remember her well: I just loved and adored her because she was so full of love. You know that feeling you get when somebody older holds you in their arms—she was that way with all the kids—a true grandmother in spirit. I wish everyone could have a grandmother like her.

I had the privilege of having two sets of loving grandparents. My mother's father was named George Phillips; my grandmother was Emma Phillips. On my father's side, my grandmother was Nely Scott and my grandfather's name was Thomas Preston Scott. They died in their late sixties, and they were in North Carolina so I didn't see them as often as my Phillips grandparents. But I loved them!

My paternal grandfather, Thomas Preston Scott, who lived in North Wilkesboro, North Carolina, worked in a grain and feed store. They sold everything for the farm. I remember how much fun it was to go with him to the store. He was a sweet man, a tall man, thin as a rail, who chewed tobacco. He had old, gnarly hands, and he used to hold my hand and take me to the feed store. To this day I still love to walk through a feed store or a farm cooperative—the images and smell of my grandfather's place always come to mind. The wheat seed, oats, molasses always smelled so good you wanted to eat 'em.

Those images, smells, and memories are an important part of me. When I'm depressed or tired I'll walk into a feed store just to experience that smell and bring back sharp memories of my Scott grandparents.

My grandfather on my mother's side, George Phillips, also from western North Carolina, moved to Maryland— near Baltimore—in 1950. He had a farm, which offered me something that I will always treasure: a link to the pioneer past of America. Even though they had one electric line in the house and electric lights and an old Frigidaire refrigerator with the compressor on top, the rest of the house was just like the 1790s. They used kerosene lamps, since the electric line had only one socket; they had a hand pump to pump water into the house; and the kitchen had a woodstove that stayed hot 365 days of the year.

Everything my grandmother cooked was made on that woodstove. My grandmother was a typical farm-family mother. She would regularly prepare dinner for thirty people, and that meant something was always cooking in the kitchen. All of my grandmother's recipes went back to her grandmother.

My grandfather worked as a dairy farmer, and he milked cows by hand until 1946, when they got an electric milker. They bought coffee and sugar and that was about all—everything else they made themselves. This was during World War II when things were rationed, but we grandkids didn't feel the effect of rations because my grandparents made their own food. They farmed enough food to last the winter: It was incredible how self-sufficient they were. We had chickens and eggs, and my grandfather grew his own wheat and had a threshing machine. They had a springhouse where they kept butter and seed. All of these things allowed me to see what life was like years ago—the way things were when *their* grandparents lived.

Going out to the hayfield with my grandfather is one of my strongest recollections. My grandfather had horses, not a tractor, on that farm, and the horses pulled everything. The rake, the sidebar—the horses pulled those. My job was to mash the hay down in the wagon. They'd take a pitchfork-full of hay, throw it up into the wagon, and I'd have to march around on it mashing it down so that they could get more hay into the wagon. Oh yes, and we always went to church on Sunday—in four cars.

It was at my grandparents' farm that I learned to drive a 1929 Ford. It didn't have any brakes, so to stop it, you had to throw it in reverse or second gear.

I remember one Halloween my grandfather kept saying, "Look out the window." It was dark, but I looked out the window and didn't see anything. Then, all of a sudden I saw this ghost go by. It was my grandmother in a sheet! Of course I knew it, but I was happy to play along.

Just thinking about times like that makes me long for those days. The memories are so sweet.

I spent almost all my summers up on that farm—I swam in the creek, and there were rope swings, or you could swing like Tarzan from vines in the trees—and it shaped my life more than anything else, even more than the house in which I was born and raised. That's why I live on a farm now, because I loved that farm so much and it was such a wonderful part of my life.

My grandparents were born somewhere around the 1870s and lived to the 1950s. Through my grandparents, I got to delve back even further into my family's past. My grandparents told me about their parents—and listening to them was like looking through a window into the 1860s.

❧ ❧

In many ways, my grandparents were as much a part of my life as my parents. I'm happy to be able to say that my parents and my wife's parents were much the same for our children.

My wife, Mary, and I were the first from both our families to give our parents grandchildren. Both sets of grandparents lived nearby and fought over who got to take the grandchildren on weekends: When they got wind that Mary and I were going to go away, they raced to make phone calls to see who would get to babysit. Having built-in babysitters is one of the greatest gifts you get from your parents. Who are you going to leave your kids with who's better and safer than their grandparents?

And the grandchildren loved having them, absolutely. Our children remember all the things they did with their grandparents, even so many years later, just as I do. Their grandparents, both sets, would love to take them for weeks at a time.

My father-in-law, Bob Dwyer—I remember how he loved to come over and pick up little Mary, the first of his grandchildren, and take her out for strolls. All of our children had a wonderful, wonderful relationship with all their grandparents, who loved them and adored them to pieces.

Now that I'm a grandfather myself, I realize that the best thing about having grandkids is that you get the kid for the best part of the ride—kind of like owning a car for only the first 10,000 miles. You can have your grandchildren for a couple of days and then turn them back over to the parents. I'm sure my grandparents felt the same way, even though they had seventeen grandchildren (pretty typical for a farm family back then).

In reality, I don't get to see my grandchildren as much as I would like to, and I think that's probably true for most grandparents today. It used to be that everyone in the same family lived in the same community and saw each other every day. So if somebody got sick, there was always someone to take care of them. Your grandparents were there to help you out, and when they needed taking care of, you were there to help them.

Today, for better or worse, families are more spread out. Grandma is in an assisted living facility in Bangor, Maine, and the kids are in Hawaii. Maybe they can manage to see each other once a year. Well, you do the best you can. Maybe it makes you sad that you can't see your grandchildren quite as much as you'd like, but then you cherish the times that you are together all the more.

Grandparents sometimes don't realize all the good things their grandchildren can learn by being with them. Through your grandparents you create the memories that become a part of the foundation of your adult life, even in those families that are spread out and don't see each other as often as they used to.

Grandparents are truly the best way to teach history to children, because they are living historians and your connection to the past. On our old family farm in North Carolina all my great-grandparents are buried on a hill. My grandparents used to take me to visit that hill and when they did, they would tell me all sorts of stories about my relatives and our family's past. As a result, I have always felt it's very beneficial to visit the graves of your ancestors with your grandparents if you can.

Knowing your grandparents gives you insight and tells you so much about yourself. Who your parents and your grandparents are has a lot to do with who you become. You can trace your own physical characteristics from your parents and grandparents, but more than that, knowing them also can tell you where you came from, spiritually and emotionally. When you can recall how your grandparents handled the tough things in their lives, you can recall the stories and their wisdom and strength to help you when you're in trouble or having a problem.

Grandparents are probably the greatest support system you can have. You know your mother and father are there for you, but behind them are the grandparents. They have the experience, which if you recognize it and use it, can be a tremendous shield as you go out and do battle in life. And you know that if you have a strong relationship with them, when something goes wrong in your life, you can go back to them and call on them, and they'll help you. We all need all the help we can get in life. Even if they're no longer with us, you can rely on your knowledge of or experiences with them to imagine how they would have handled the problem.

But of course the greatest benefit of having grandparents—and also of being a grandparent—is the love grandparents and grandchildren naturally have for each other. The love that grandparents have for their grandchildren is plain in everything they do.

You know, you can't love your grandchildren too much, and there's no such thing as spending too much time with them. Grandparents can have an incredible influence on their grandchildren. Grandchildren watch what you do, they store it away in their memories, and pick up on your good traits . . . and your bad. Always remember that. They'll emulate you, so you want to be worthy of their emulation.

But you know what? Even if you're not the best grandparent you could possibly be, even if you can't visit as often as you'd like, even if you'd like the grandchildren to be a little less messy or a little more respectful, it's still great being family. That's the theme here—the love we have for each other. That's the most important thing you can have.

I love being a grandparent so much that I wanted to share the joys I found by being one. In my last book, *The Older the Fiddle, the Better the Tune*, I shared my reflections on getting older but staying young at heart. And I got such wonderful friends to share their experiences, wisdom, and insight, too. So I thought I would ask some more of my friends about the joys they experience by either being a grandparent or spending time with one. What you'll read are many fond memories, touching stories, and very funny encounters. I was so happy to learn that there are so many people that not only adore their grandparents, but also love being one. I hope you enjoy reading this collection as much as I did.

Brian Aldiss

Brian W. Aldiss is a writer whose science fiction work has brought him his greatest fame. Additionally, his poems, plays, essays, and other novels have marked him as one of the most versatile and influential writers of our time.

A question often asked is: "What is the purpose of human beings here on Earth?" Some people have a religious answer, that we are somehow working out God's plan, as if He were a master chess player. That is as it may be. More certainly, we are here to propagate our species. This is what gives us most gratification.

Of recent years, breeding times have been much extended. Basically, however, the situation remains the same as it ever was: we grow to reproductive age, we reproduce, and then we fall off the perch.

Although we cannot exactly be happy about that fall, the drop is eased if we have children to carry on our name. Some of us, the more long-lived, may see not only grandchildren, but also our great-grandchildren. So the long chain of our genes extends into the future.

My good fortune is to have a boy and a girl by my first marriage and a boy and a girl by my second marriage. I regard this as the natural order of things: "Whatever is, is right," in the words of Alexander Pope.

Even better, these four remarkable people—they are all fully grown by now, of course—get on well together and are of happy and equable disposition. All have partners; three of the four are married and so far two of them, the older pair, have three boys between them—my clever and lively grandchildren. Much as I love them, I am a bit too old to enter into their outdoor games. And much as I love them, I could never possibly love them as greatly as I love my four dear children, who taught me so much by their entry into the world and their growing up.

Buzz Aldrin

Buzz Aldrin is a former NASA astronaut. On July 20, 1969, he and Neil Armstrong became the first humans to walk on the moon.

I've had the privilege of sending my grandson, Jeffrey, to various space camps across the country in recent summers, and each time I can't help but consider the incredible innovations and changes that have taken place since I was sent off to Trout Lake Camp as a young boy.

My generation witnessed the rise of airpower, the launching of satellites, and even the landing of men on the moon. We've fought through devastating world wars and witnessed the rise and fall of great nations. Etched in stone monuments and memorials are the names of countless men and women who have sacrificed everything for the freedoms we enjoy. I try to share these stories with my grandson as often as I can.

Despite all of these advancements, much has remained the same. Though Jeffrey's generation will face challenges wholly different and in some ways more terrible than our own, it does so with the same freedoms that its grandparents had, and with that freedom this generation is the inheritor of unlimited possibilities.

As I see Jeffrey off to space camp, I am proud and thrilled that I might be sending off a future astronaut. But regardless of where my grandson ends up, I hope that he remembers the dedication and sacrifice of two generations ago, and the responsibility that is this legacy of freedom that we have left him.

❧ ❦

Jane Alexander

Jane Alexander is an actress who has been nominated for three Academy Awards and has appeared in such classic films as All the President's Men *and* Kramer vs. Kramer. *She served as chairperson of the National Endowment for the Arts from 1993 until 1997.*

*I*sabelle, age four, is severely restricted by my son and daughter-in-law in the amount of sugar she eats. They were visiting us for ten days in our summer home, where the rules are always more relaxed. On the last morning of their stay as I was alone in the kitchen cooking breakfast, little Isabelle came quietly downstairs and said somberly, "Oh, Nana, I will miss you and Pushkie [her name for her Grandpa] sooo much."

My heart swelled, and then she added, "But I realize I will not have my Honey Nut Cheerios anymore."

I almost burst out laughing, then seeing how serious her look was I asked instead, "Sugar is really your favorite thing, isn't it?"

"Yes, my favorite thing in the whole wide world," she replied.

"Hmmm," I said, "if you had to choose between your mother and sugar, which would it be?"

There was a long Jack Benny pause (remember the old "Your money or your life" routine?), and then she yelled, "Sugar!"

Then she collapsed in a flurry of giggles and added, "Just kidding."

Jayne Meadows Allen

Jayne Meadows Allen, an Emmy Award winner, has appeared on Broadway, television, and film. She has also co-starred opposite the legendary Steve Allen, her husband of almost fifty years, in their multi-award-winning historical series "Meeting of Minds."

Saintly Elizabeth Meadows, my paternal grandmother, is the role model I have attempted to emulate with my three adored grandchildren, nine step-grandchildren, and five step great-grandchildren.

At ten years of age, I wrote a play a month. It was always the same plot, only the costumes and props changed.

In every play I cast my sister, Audrey, as the lovely princess, keeping the best part, the melodramatic witch, for myself.

Our audience of two consisted of our English bulldog, Pal, and dear grandmother, who sat patiently, month after month, applauding enthusiastically although she had heard not a word. Grandmother was stone deaf from birth.

Most of us suffer, occasionally, from emotional homelessness and, oh, how I needed the encouragement and unconditional love of that sensitive lady, a love I enjoy sharing today with my darlings, since each has uniquely different needs.

Eighteen-year-old Bradley, my first grandchild, offered recently to drive me to a very glamorous party for the cast of the Oscar-winning movie *Chicago*. My neighbors, Patty and Dick Van Patten, had promised to bring me home. Brad asked if he could come inside to say "Hi" to Dick. The "Hi" turned into: "Are you sure, Mr. Van Patten, that it's not inconvenient for you to drive my grandmother home tonight?" Adding, with a twinkle in his eye, "Please make sure, sir, that she's home by a decent hour." At six feet two inches, Bradley is my trusted bodyguard and the heart of the Allen family.

Sixteen-year-old Bobby, a Steve Allen clone, is the humor of the family. He and I attend tap classes and the theater together and of course we talk show biz until it's coming out of our ears. One of my greatest joys is coaching Bob in his high school plays and preparing him for some of the inevitable heartbreaks that face the life of an actor. He will appear this summer in a rock opera at the Edinburgh International Festival in Scotland. I shall be front and center.

And then there's seven-year-old Amanda Michelle, who was always the apple of Grandpa Steve's eye and, of course, the romance of the family. Recently, we were all enjoying dinner together at our favorite Chinese restaurant and after dessert, were reading aloud our fortune cookies. Amanda read hers: "Soon someone you love very much will come to see you." Without a second's hesitation, she leapt from her chair, hugged the fortune to her chest, and squealed, "Oh boy, Grandpa Steve's coming back!"

Out of the mouths of babes.

My rules for grandparenting:

A. Be available.

B. Never criticize!

C. Be as genuinely interested in their dreams as in a skinned knee.

☙ ❧

Roger Armstrong

Roger Armstrong is an award-winning cartoonist and painter. He is a former Walt Disney Company staff artist whose work includes the Ella Cinders, Napoleon and Uncle Elby, Little Lulu, *and* Scamp *comic strips.*

*W*hen my granddaughter Christina was a little girl of seven or eight, she loved to hang over my drawing board to watch me draw. It was 1958 and I was producing the *Napoleon* comic strip, which, at that time, was distributed by the *L.A. Times* newspaper syndicate. Christina was the second child of my (step) daughter Mignon—who, with her sister Karen, lived near us in San Gabriel, California.

At the time, I didn't think much of her diligent attention to my activity. She would watch me work while her siblings frantically played outside. Christina was my favorite grandchild (at that time I only had a few—later I had lots) and we would talk a lot while she watched me draw.

Okay, fast forward—

Fifty plus years have gone speeding by. Now I'm retired—well, not exactly retired; I'm an art teacher and conduct classes four days a week. I haven't done any comic strips for the past twelve years (the last strip I drew was *Scamp*

for the Walt Disney Company). Now I teach drawing and painting in my studio as well as in various art schools.

And what has happened to Christina? Well, she is now a top-notch graphic designer and head of the graphic design department at Saddleback College in Mission Viejo, California, where she also teaches. She takes excellent care of her grandfather, driving him to various engagements as required since he doesn't drive at night anymore.

"Did the many hours you spent as a child watching me draw comics have any influence on your career decision?" I asked her one day. "Are you kidding?" she said. "Of course they did."

And so it goes, one generation transfers to the next, for the most part, inadvertently.

We humans are eclectic on almost every level. We learn—and build on—all that we gathered from those who preceded us; none of us "spring full blown from the brow of Zeus."

Grandparenting is an ongoing joy, especially when one is able to participate, as I can, in the obvious continuity.

Christina, as well as Michael, her son, now thirty-two years old, is living proof that "life goes on."

The presence of a grandparent confirms that parents were, indeed, little once, too, and that people who are little can grow to be big, can become parents, and one day even have grandchildren of their own. So often we think of grandparents as belonging to the past; but in this important way, grandparents, for young children, belong to the future.

—FRED ROGERS

Dick Ayers

Dick Ayers is a comic book artist who has been penciling, lettering, inking, and coloring since 1948. Some of his most famous titles include Sgt. Fury *and* Ghost Rider.

Yes, if I had known grandchildren were so much fun, I would have had them first! I have been very fortunate as a comic book artist working at home and being able to share the many visits they had at their grandparents' home. My first grandchild was Lauren. We shared many "firsts" together. One always brings joy when I highlight its memory. Lauren was four years old—a gorgeous, cute red-haired girl, and I brought her with me to Manhattan on the train

A MEMORY OF FOUR GRANDCHILDREN —
LAUREN, JAMES, KIMBERLY AND KARA
AND THREE GREAT-GRANDCHILDREN
MEGHAN, GRIFFIN AND CONNOR
AND GRANDMA "CHARLIE" WATCHING GRANDPA
DRAW A COMIC BOOK STORY...

from White Plains, New York—her first trip to "the city." At Grand Central Station, I hailed a taxi on Vanderbilt Avenue to proceed to Warner Communications up by the Radio City skating rink. As the taxi proceeded on 45th Street, I pointed out to Lauren, "See, Lauren, all the buildings?!" and she answered, "See all the people, Grandpa!" The taxi driver interjected: "Wow, that little girl is smart, mister! She knows what is important!"

Grandchildren *are* very special. Perhaps that's why they are called "grand" children. And we "grand" parents are grand to them, too. Their grandmother and I celebrated our fiftieth anniversary in 2001 with a gathering of relatives, friends, and neighbors and, as a tribute, Lauren stood center-stage and read a poem she wrote citing the grandchildren's memories. It begins

> *Together we gather in celebration for*
> *Fifty years of marriage complete.*
> *A couple, a family, many*
> *Generations toast this marvelous feat.*
> *You may know them as Dick & Lindy,*
> *Richard & Charlotte, Mr. & Mrs. Ayers.*
> *Charlie and Grandpa, they are to us,*
> *But we all can agree, they are quite a pair.*

There are six stanzas of their memories of the times shared with us and she closes with

A grandchild never felt so loved and
This is our anniversary wish to you.
May you know how much your love
Means, how honest it is and true.
May you cherish each other for
Many days and view the pictures on your wall.
For we are all the family that you
Created, gathered here one and all!

LOVE, LAUREN & JAMIE

Lindy and I were blessed with five grandchildren: Lauren, James, Kimberly, Kara, and Christopher, our step-grandson. Today we are blessed with three great-grandchildren and are having fun getting to know Meghan, Griffin, and Connor. Already I'm looking forward to bobsledding with Griffin, who will be two years old this winter. I am most fortunate. I can still do some of the things I did with our children, Elaine, Stephen, Richard, and Frederick.

The closest friends I have made all through life have been people who also grew up close to a loved and living grandmother or grandfather.

—MARGARET MEAD

Howard Baker, Jr.

Howard H. Baker, Jr., served three terms as a United States senator from Tennessee from 1967 until 1985. He was appointed the United States Ambassador to Japan in June of 2001 by President George W. Bush.

*W*hen my second grandson, Matthew, was about eight years old, I took him to Channel 5 in Nashville to do one of those feature pieces that television does often and does well. He listened attentively to everything like a fine young gentleman. On the way home in the car, he looked at me and said, "Papa, did you used to be somebody?"

As is often the case with a question from a grandson, it was unanswerable.

Kaye Ballard

Kaye Ballard is an actress and singer. She debuted on the screen in 1957 in The Girl Most Likely *and went on to star in* The Mothers-in-Law *and* The Steve Allen Comedy Hour *on television.*

*M*y grandmother was the most important and influential person in my life. I left home at seventeen because I thought she was going to die, and I wanted to get used to living without her. She lived another forty years! She was the greatest influence in my life.

Rik Battaglia

Rik Battaglia is an Italian actor who has performed in a wide variety of international films since the 1950s, including the original Wild Wild West *and* Treasure Island.

I have two granddaughters and one grandson from three different families; the oldest one is twenty-eight years old, the middle one is fourteen, and the little boy is five years old. We cherish the joy they give us, but we receive these little pleasures only as long as they look spontaneously for our hand to be accompanied where they want to go and from then onwards it remains only a happy memory. *Ca c'est la vie.*

When kids are small, they are so sweet you could eat them. As they grow, you regret you did not do so.

Betsy Blair

Betsy Blair began her acting career in the 1940s. One of her most memorable roles, Clara Snyder in Marty *(1955), merited her Best Actress Awards at the Cannes Film Festival and the British Film Academy and an Oscar nomination for Best Supporting Actress. She has recently written her autobiography,* The Memory of All That: Love and Politics in New York, Hollywood, and Paris. *She is a supporter of Amnesty International.*

MY BABY'S BABY

. . . *C*rowed my mother, albeit tearfully. My daughter had just been born.

I was an eighteen-year-old, white, healthy, married, middle-class American, overflowed with joy, awe, exhaustion, pride—every new-mother feeling.

Even so, as my own eyes filled in response to my mother's tears, my snippy adolescent self was thinking, "How sweet she is—but how silly and sentimental she is."

Boy, was I wrong!

The years pass. I was a happy wife and mother. Then I was an unhappy wife and still a happy mother; then divorced as a happy mother; then remarried to my eternal happiness as a wife, mother, stepmother.

Looking back, I can assess the core of my happiness as being the unchanging love for my daughter. She is the continuous strand in my life. Work and love and friends have an ebb and flow; a child is forever.

So I don't think I was surprised at the power of my feelings when my daughter was pregnant for the first time. I had renewed visions of her round, smooth little arms and tiny fingernails. In my dreams, I reheard her gurgles and saw her first steps. Her baby clothes that I had saved came out of the tissue paper to be washed and ironed. The grandmother's part in building the nest to welcome the newcomer to the family was being assembled, twig by twig.

And then came Rebecca. She was beautiful; my daughter Kerry, her mother, was beautiful; her husband, Jack, the father, was beautiful. It was a beautiful day.

As for me, my eyes filling with tears as I held Rebecca in my arms, I found myself loving my own mother. She had been a sensational grandmother. Could I do as well? Her words, "my baby's baby," were rollicking gleefully around inside my head. I couldn't say them aloud—I still thought they were corny. But I saw, with absolute clarity, the difference between sentiment and sentimentality. It is a distinction we make in discussing art, movies, plays, music. My mother was not silly or sentimental; she was loving, full of sentiment, and not afraid to show it, not afraid to say her "corny" words out loud.

I did have enormous fun being a mother, but being a grandmother is different. All the clichés are true. Grandchildren give you joy without hardship; and as people say, grandchildren go home when you're tired. To that I reply, although I'm a city girl, I wish we lived in a village where I'd see them every day, where going home didn't sometimes involve airplanes.

Inevitably, there are some difficult moments as an infant becomes an adult: the moments when we adjust our lives to being parents; the terrible moments of fear when a child is hurt or ill; the seemingly endless moments of conflict that come with adolescence.

As a grandparent, you have been there. You are proof that these moments pass. Without doing anything spectacular, you are given your place in the great river of love that rushes underground through the generations and nourishes them.

And newborn grandchildren seem to know this in some mysterious way. They love you for nothing. They run and jump into your arms; they can be comforted and fall asleep clutching your finger or nestled against you. The aesthetic perfection of their tiny bodies is an endless consolation. Your own grey hair or crinkly arms disappear when you gaze on their shining locks and smooth skin. They give you reality. They show you the meaning of life by tumbling you into that river of love.

I'm lucky. I have seven of them. My daughter gave us two more: Ben and Anna. My stepsons and their wives gave us four: Julian, Milo, Theo, and Francesca. Each one brings beauty and wit and joy to the world. Each one is a distinct and original human being.

My dear husband, who died last year, was a profoundly happy grandfather. He and his brother lost almost all their family in the Holocaust: parents, grandparents, uncles, aunts, cousins. For them, the birth of their grandchildren, their very existence, brought them not only the joys I feel but much, much more. Through their children, they found a great deal of what they had lost; they had re-created a family. And their grandchildren? They are their life's blood, a living, human-scale miracle. Hooray for people—especially grandchildren.

P.S. Rebecca, my first grandchild, is about to get married. If I'm lucky, I'll be a great-grandmother. Hooray again!

Joseph Bonsall

Joseph S. Bonsall is a thirty-year member of The Oak Ridge Boys. *He is also the author of the* Molly the Cat *children's book series, as well as the inspirational novel* G.I. Joe & Lillie. *His latest book,* The Oak Ridge Boys: American Journey, *is forthcoming.*

BRE AND LUKE

I glance around the Chuck E. Cheese's and notice that my fifty-five years makes me the oldest person in the place. Along with about sixty or seventy children running back and forth between video games and such, I see mostly young mommies or daddies in their twenties or early thirties.

All of these young parents seem to possess that same tired look that I see in the eyes of my oldest daughter. Raising kids is not for the lazy or the squeamish. You cannot begin to match their energy level, but you always have to figure out a way to keep up with them.

I take a bite of pizza. Hmmmmm, not a bad pie.

"Pop Pop, come here and look," yells a handsome, little four-year-old boy who has just mastered a game wherein some animals pop up out of holes and he hits them on the head with a hammer. It just takes one token, and as Pop Pop has provided him with a whole cup of tokens, these poor creatures are really in for some trouble.

BONK . . .

"Owwwwwww, HAHAHA!" Nothing like the laughter of a grandson.

"Cool, Luke, you are really good at that one, look at all the tickets you are winning," I exclaim as I watch a beaver take a hit. BAM!

You see, each game awards the children tickets that can be redeemed on the way out for all kinds of little toys and gifts . . . which brings me to Breanne. At age eight, she is simply beautiful. The walking image of her mother, Sabrina, and her Mom Mom, my Mary. It's amazing to see the women I love so represented in the life force of my granddaughter.

Bre is playing Skee-Ball. Good old Skee-Ball, a game that hasn't changed in a hundred years. Roll the ball down the little alleyway, up it flies, eventually landing in one of several holes, each one progressively harder to get. The more difficult holes award more cumulative points and Bre is racking up tickets.

"I am really, really good, huh, Pop Pop?" Bre smiles. (Hello, Mary. Hello, Sabrina.)

"You are the best, Hon. Are you guys finished eating?" I yell loud enough for Luke to hear.

"I am full, Pop Pop." BONK. "Oowwwww," Luke yells with glee.

"Yes! Yes! Yes!" says Breanne. "One more game though, okay?"

Okay! I start to gather up all of their tickets, and we eventually make our way to the little redemption center at the front of Chuck E. Cheese's. A very cool place really. Good food, lots of games, children running around and laughing. A little carnival by the mall. As John Mellencamp might say, "Ain't that America!"

Between the three of us (I did shoot some hoops and earned a few myself), we have about 280 tickets. Plenty enough for a space gun for Luke, but well short of what was required for a Barbie Make-Up Kit. I grab Breanne before she heads back for the Skee-Ball game and proceed to negotiate with a young eighteen-year-old behind the counter who has a pin sticking through her nose. Miss Pierce eventually sells me the Barbie kit and everyone is happy.

Especially me. You see, I am a man of the road and over all of these years I have missed a lot of good, home stuff. I am not complaining, for God has blessed me with a great career, and I have always believed that for everything worthwhile there is always a price to be paid. My sacrifice has been missing a lot of quality time with my daughters, Jennifer and Sabrina.

Now I am a grandfather taking two beautiful children to Chuck E. Cheese's and then to a movie about a talking mouse. Pop Pop is on cloud nine. We sing and tell jokes as we drive around town.

"You know why there is a fence around the cemetery?" I ask.

Bre and Luke scream the answer together as one, "BECAUSE PEOPLE ARE DYING TO GET IN THERE!"

"You know how many people are dead in there?"

"ALL OF THEM!"

More laughter and carrying on.

I finally pull into the driveway of their home where mommy and daddy are waiting to put the two very sleepy kids to bed. I drive off amazed at how many sour gummy worms a four-year-old boy can eat during one movie, especially after pizza at Chuck E. Cheese's.

The cell phone rings. It is Mom Mom. "How did it go?"

"Just great, Hon, just great! I'll be home soon."

Often Mary and I take the grandkids out together but tonight it had been decided that just Pop Pop should take them and, as always, my time with these children is never forgotten. Each memory is as clear as crystal.

You haven't lived until you ride around in big circles on a John Deere tractor with a little grandchild fast asleep on your lap. Taking them fishing, or to a movie, or playing catch, or a game of checkers or Trouble can be as refreshing as a summer rain. Being a grandparent allows you to spoil them rotten and then . . . take them home. That is all part of the Great Plan, I guess, and it certainly works for Mary and me. You should see Christmas!

After arriving back home I cannot help reflecting back upon the circle of time that is passing before me. Two empty bedrooms now exist where once slept the two beautiful little girls who grew up under our own watch.

My Jennifer, who is now twenty-nine, and my Sabrina, who is thirty-three, have turned into two wonderful and responsible young women who, thankfully, each married a strong, sturdy, and hard-working all-American boy. And for all of this, I am very thankful.

Jen lives in Florida and is now a vice president of a cutting edge marketing firm, and Sabrina, who lives right here in Tennessee, is an interior designer, as well as being mommy to Bre and Luke.

The responsibility of bringing up Bre and Luke does not rest with Mary and me. We are on the periphery, as we should be, lending support and help when needed and, quite frankly, enjoying all the good parts.

However, the same old worries still exist. *Will they be healthy? Will they be sane? Will they survive driving and college and fads and friends? Will they make something positive out of their opportunity to live in America or will they be a constant heartbreak to their parents?*

As a father, I have been through this process already and, let's face it, there is just so much that we can do. The rest is always a crapshoot and, hopefully, God in His infinite wisdom is guiding the roll of the dice. As a Pop Pop, I constantly ask God to protect these little ones who are now a part of my life. One day, a few years back, I received some very positive direction, and it came from my grand-daughter.

When Breanne was a few months shy of turning three years old, we had a conversation that I will never forget as long as I live, a conversation that brings me comfort to this very day. We were sitting on the floor of her bedroom and she was describing for me, in a very serious fashion, the different creatures who lived under her bed and in her closet. I was fascinated.

"Daddy says that it is just my imagination, but I can see them all quite clearly, Pop Pop," she said.

"Well, spirits and beings do exist, Bre, ummmm, the Bible even says that they do," I answered.

"They are real, Pop Pop, and I can see them!" she insisted.

She proceeded to explain their colors and shapes and demeanors, and I found myself totally absorbed. I had never had a conversation like this in my entire life and I felt honored that she was sharing her heart with me.

A few quiet moments passed.

"Are any of these guys bad?" I asked.

"Some are!"

"Do you get scared of them?"

"Nope! You see, Pop Pop, nothing can hurt me because of the Angel. He protects me. He is from God." She was smiling now and looking so beautiful.

"Is he in the room now?" I asked, as my spine tingled just a bit.

She whispered, as if sharing a secret, "I can't always see him, Pop Pop, but he told me that he is always here for me . . . and I believe him."

Then so do I.

May God always keep a watchful eye on Bre and Luke.

The feeling of grandparents for their grandchildren can be expressed this way: "Our children are dear to us; but when we have grandchildren, they seem to be more dear than our children were." You might say that the grandmother falls all over herself to try to show her appreciation for her grandchild. It goes right back to those wishes that were made for them when they were little girls: the wish that they would live to become grandmothers someday.

—HENRY OLD COYOTE

Willard on What
My Grandchildren
Taught Me
about Myself

. . . . . .

It's okay to get on all fours and crawl around the floor, no matter how old you are.

I never lost my ability to enjoy new things—and to seek them out.

I did a great job parenting my own kids.

E-mail is my friend. I've made it this far; I can learn to use a computer.

Slowing down and enjoying is what life is about.

Art Buchwald

Art Buchwald is a nationally syndicated humorist and author of over twenty books, including the best-selling memoirs Leaving Home *and* I'll Always Have Paris. *He was awarded the Pulitzer Prize for Outstanding Commentary in 1982.*

Grandchildren are so much fun—except when they run out of money. First they use up all their parents' dough and then they work on their grandparents.

Outside of that, they are more interesting than their parents because you don't have to take any guff from them. The best time to see a grandchild is at graduation. The worst time is when he has stayed out all night.

As for granddaughters, they always butter you up.

Love is the only thing grandchildren can give you, and the only thing you can give them.

Dan Burton

Dan Burton is a United States representative from Indiana. He serves as the chairman of the House Government Reform Subcommittee on Human Rights and Wellness.

Grandkids are great because you can spoil them rotten and then send them home and repay your children for all the heartburn they caused you when they were little!

George H. W. Bush

George H. W. Bush was the forty-first president of the United States of America. His son, George W. Bush, went on to be the forty-third president.

An excerpt from his book, All the Best, George Bush: My Life and Other Writings, *appears below:*

𝒟ecember 31, 1989

It's been some year—a fascinating year of change. I end the year with more confidence, and end the year with real gratitude to our team. They've pulled together. They had very little individual grandstanding. . . .

I'm certainly not seen as a visionary, but I hope I'm seen as steady and prudent and able.

The tough thing was going down early in my Presidency to speak at the ceremony for the *Iowa* sailors. I've gotten a little better at that at year's end, but not very good. When something close and personal happens, I break up and I know it. I couldn't speak at Fred Chamber's funeral. . . .

Bar's been sick this year,[1] but she's as strong as she can be, though her eyes bother her. She's captured the imagination of the country, and it's wonderful. My worries are about her eyes—they hurt her. They're changing the medication, etc., but she'll do fine. I'm sure of that—she's got to. . . .

One of the greatest highlights was the day after Christmas. I was getting ready to go to the office, and Ellie—beautiful Ellie, who lights up any room she's in—said, "Gampy, come here," so I went into the bathroom. She pointed into the toilet, and said, "Did you leave that poopoo?" Not many people would talk to the President of the United States like that.

* * *

[1]Bar was diagnosed with Graves' disease, which affects the thyroid, but she was doing better on medicine.

One of life's greatest mysteries is how the boy who
wasn't good enough to marry your daughter can be
the father of the smartest grandchild in the world.

—JEWISH PROVERB

Benjamin Cardin

*Benjamin L. Cardin is a United States representative from
the 3rd Congressional District in Maryland, a position he has
held since 1987. He is a member of the Ways and Means
Committee as well as the Budget Committee.*

I could not agree with you more that one of the greatest
gifts of being a parent is the joy of grandchildren. In fact,
on the day I received your letter requesting my participation in your book project, my second granddaughter—
Julia Helen Willis—was born.

While I am sure that Julia will be as brilliant and able
as her sister Madeline, I have spent more than three years

as Madeline's grandfather and I have a number of funny anecdotes about our first grandchild.

Madeline is a bright and self-assured three-and-a-half-year-old. She is very feminine and very aware of others around her. In fact, this summer I took Madeline to a Little League game at the White House. In greeting those who were there, President Bush made a special effort to say hello to Madeline and ask if she was having a good time. Madeline very politely responded, "Yes, thank you."

After the president had walked away, Madeline turned to me and asked, "Who was that?" Needless to say, manners aside, Madeline didn't fully appreciate her conversation with President Bush.

Madeline is delighted in her new little sister and is awaiting the day that she can lead the way for Julia in such important social occasions as visiting the White House.

I don't know who my grandfather was; I am much more concerned to know what his grandson will be.

—ABRAHAM LINCOLN

Eugene Cernan

Eugene A. Cernan is a former astronaut. He participated in the Gemini IX, Apollo X, *and* Apollo XVII *space missions, and in 1966 became the second American to walk in space. He is now chairman and CEO of The Cernan Corporation and a National Aviation Hall of Fame enshrinee. Excerpts from his autobiography,* The Last Man on the Moon, *appear below.*

POPPIE'S MOON

*M*y favorite times today take place at the ranch, whether feeding my longhorns or getting mud-filthy digging post holes. With a fire crackling in the stone hearth at the end of the open porch on a cool evening, Jan and I watch the deer come down to drink from the ponds and graze unafraid among the cattle. Our three Labs sprawl in a lazy pile, and grandchildren prowl about. The feeling is idyllic.

It was on one such evening that I watched the Moon rise full and achingly bright. When I see it like that, I can instantly transport myself back to the valley I once called home, a place where I had a house, a job, a car and commuted to work. The Sun bathes the boulders and massifs, and I again tingle with the absolute stillness and understand the presence of our Earth in the heavens. The crisp memories are not unlike those of childhood, such as the barn and cornfields of Grandpa's farm, or when Mom and Dad would take my sister and me on vacations to places of which we had only dreamed. Some things are no less real just because they belong to the distant past.

On this evening, as the Moon climbed slowly above the hills, I scooped my five-year-old granddaughter Ashley into my arms, just as I had once held her mother, Tracy, beneath a similar night sky. I thought that now perhaps she was old enough to understand, to remember, and I prepared to tell her the story.

But before I could speak, she pointed straight up, and declared in an excited voice, "Poppie, there's your moon!" She had always called it that, never knowing why.

"Do you know how far away the Moon is, Punk?" I asked.

She seemed puzzled, for a child of that age could not possibly grasp such a distance, so I rambled on, using words familiar to her. "It's way, way far away in the sky, out where God lives," I said. "Poppie flew his rocket up there and lived on that Moon for three whole days. I even wrote your mommy's initials in the sand."

Ashley gazed at it a little while longer, then lowered her eyes to meet mine, and she saw not some mighty suited-up space hero from an age before she was born, but only her silver-haired grandfather. Insects and animals were beginning their night song and a few antelope scurrying among the shadows drew her attention. She wiggled, growing anxious because she wanted to give the horses a carrot before going to bed. But she glanced up again then back at me. "Poppie," she said, "I didn't know you went to Heaven."

I felt a jolt, almost an electrical surge, as I considered her statement. Her innocent view of life unlocked the riddle that had puzzled me for so many years. My space voyages were not just about the Moon, but something much richer and deeper—the meaning of my life, weighed not only by facts from my brain, but also by the feelings from my soul. For a moment, I was again standing on another world, watching our blue Earth turn in the sable blackness of space. *Too much logic. Too much purpose. Too beautiful to have happened by accident.* My destiny was to be not only an explorer, but a messenger from outer space, an apostle for the future.

Too many years have passed for me to still be the last man to have walked on the Moon. Somewhere on Earth today is the young girl or boy, the possessor of indomitable will and courage, who will lift that dubious honor from me and take us back out there where we belong.

Listen. Let me tell you what it was like . . .

I gave Ashley a big squeeze. She had just bathed and smelled fresh and clean and alive, her baby powder so much more enchanting than the distant, dusty perfume of the goddess Luna. I have a wonderful set of yesterdays. Jan, my kids, and the grandchildren are the promise of tomorrow.

"Yes, Punk," I carried the laughing girl over to the corral. "Your Poppie went to heaven. He really did."

If nothing is going well, call your grandmother.

—ITALIAN PROVERB

Al Cervi

Al Cervi is a basketball player and coach who was inducted into the Basketball Hall of Fame in 1985. Known for his hustle and his ability to lead a team, he was both a player and the coach of the Syracuse Nationals for five years. He retired from both with a winning record.

The following reflections were written by one of Al Cervi's four grandchildren. Here, Lauren, age ten, shares thoughts on her grandmother and grandfather for class assignments.

A POEM

BY LAUREN CERVI

My grandpa is a very hard worker,
But he always has time for fun.
Sometimes he teases me, but I know
He still loves me by two ton.

Whatever he does,
He must do it right.
Sometimes when I try to and do it wrong,
We get into a fight.

Weather [sic] we get along or fight,
He's always my number one pal.
He's the best friend a girl could have,
And his name is Al!

THE BULL FISH AND THE BEST GRANDMA
by Lauren Cervi

I will never forget the time when I caught a bull fish. I couldn't get it off my hook. It all happened like this. I was in the Adirondacks. My mom, aunt, and grandpa were not home, but my grandma was. I wanted to go fishing. So my grandma said she'd come and watch me, as long as she did not have to take a fish off the hook! I knew how so I said she did not have to. We went down to the dock. I caught about two sunfish, then I caught a bull fish. I waved my rod in the water. I did not want to take it off myself! I was afraid it would prick me! My grandpa does it all the time. The bull fish came off!

Then I put my rod back into the water, I got another bull fish! This time when I waved it, it did not come off! I reeled it up. I did not know what to do. I did not want to kill it, but I might have to! My grandma said she would not touch fish unless she was sitting down to eat it! I put the rod back into the water and began to cry. I took it up from the water again. I sat down and cried harder. I kept on checking to see if it was still alive. I went into the house and got a knife and I tried to cut the string; it did not come off. My grandma said that if I got some paper or something, she would try to get it off. So I got some paper. I turned and just as I was going up the stairs that led from the water, I heard my grandma yell, "Got it!" I ran back to the fishing dock. She was holding the fish in the paper. She said, "What do I do with it?" I said, very excitedly, "Drop into the water!" She dropped the fish into the water then she dropped the paper into the trash. I gave her a big hug! Later she said her hand smelled like fish.

A man's destination is his own village,
His own cooking fire, and his wife's cooking;
To sit in front of his own door at sunset
And see his grandson, and his neighbor's grandson
Playing in the dust together.

—T. S. ELIOT

Chubby Checker

Chubby Checker is a musician who was first signed to a Philadelphia recording label in 1959. Born Ernest Evans in

Spring Gulley, South Carolina, he went on to record over thirty chart-topping songs. His remake of the Hank Ballard song "The Twist" is still a staple of American dance music.

I was so amazed when I saw my children having children. I realized then that they were my journey to everlasting (watching their children as I watched them). The pages of my days are rapidly turning as I watch them play and hear them say, "Where is my granddad?" I hear their words and I hear my voice uttering the same words for the safety that my grandfather's presence gave me. Now it's my turn. How warm, how wonderful, how indescribable are the children that my children gave me.

Grandchildren are God's way of compensating us for growing old.

—MARY H. WALDRIP

Roy Clark

Roy Clark bridges the gap between singer, instrumentalist, and comedian. Perhaps best known for his role as the cohost of Hee Haw, *he is also a famous country music performer and has been a member of the Grand Ole Opry since 1987.*

*I*t doesn't seem that long ago that I was the grandchild, now I'm the grandpa. I have been blessed with three beautiful grandchildren and a fourth one is on the way! Two call me "Pop Pop" and the other calls me "Grandpa," but whatever they call me makes me feel special.

I think the proudest part of being a grandfather is when you look at your grandchildren and realize that through them, your life goes on. When you were raising your children you were so busy trying to make a living and create a life for your family that it seemed like there was never enough time to do all the things you wanted. Now, thank God, through our grandchildren, we get a second chance.

Someone once said, "the beauty of grandchildren is that they go home at night." Big words, not true. When they come up and put their little arms around you and say, "I love you Pop Pop or Grandpa," time stands still.

It's one of nature's ways that we often feel closer to distant generations than to the generation immediately preceding us.

—IGOR STRAVINSKY

Charles Colson

Chuck Colson is the founder of Prison Fellowship Ministries, an organization that works with hundreds of churches of various denominations to reach out to prison inmates and their families.

I have five grandchildren. They've been a joy to me from the first day each one was born. One is a freshman at the University of Pennsylvania; two are students at the University of Georgia; one is a very precocious student in the fifth grade; and another is in a special learning school because he, Max, is autistic.

Each in his own way is a delight. When each one of my grandchildren has gone off to their freshman year of college, I've had an opportunity to sit and talk with them. I know what they're going to run into when they get to campus. In this postmodern era, they will be told there is no truth, that everybody's preferences are as good as anyone else's. They will be taught to question the roots of their own Western culture, and that tolerance means that sometimes you never say anything that anyone else can be offended by (which is of course a formula for never saying anything, a complete distortion of the classical meaning of tolerance).

What has been a special joy in my life is when I've received calls from those grandchildren in college asking me my opinion on how to deal with a particular question raised by a professor. That makes grandpa feel smart and wanted.

Someone asked me which one of my grandchildren I love the most. I of course love them all equally as I love my three children equally. At any given moment, I love the one the most that needs it the most. That's generally Max, my twelve-year-old autistic grandson. He struggles with things that most of us take for granted, but he's a wonderful, loving kid. When Max visits me, I sit him in my office chair and he bounces up and down, gleefully exclaiming, "Grandpa's chair, grandpa's chair, grandpa's chair." Those are the moments that make being a grandfather really special.

Max will never be able to care for himself, but my daughter believes that he is perfect because he is exactly the way God made him, and he has brought untold joy and blessings into the lives of everybody he's met. Our worth in society is not always judged by our abilities and position and stature; it's judged by whether we reflect the joy of our Creator. Max is a very special little guy.

It's one of the great paradoxes of life, isn't it, that we want our children to be perfect and our grandchildren to be perfect and finish number one in spelling bees and debating contests and football games. Along comes a severely handicapped child, and he turns out to be the greatest blessing.

Nellie Connally

Nellie Connally is a former First Lady of Texas. Her husband, the late John B. Connally, was governor of Texas from 1963 to 1968. In recent years, she has devoted her time to fund-raising for breast cancer research and promoting breast cancer education.

$\mathcal{R}$eporters have asked me, "When John came home from a hard day, was in a bad humor and mad at the world, what did you do?" Well, I produced a grandchild if I could. When that little grandchild climbed into his lap, put those wonderful, chubby little arms around his neck, and gave him a big wet kiss, John forgot all his problems and enjoyed some of the sweetest love there is. You can replace a lot of things, but never a grandchild. We have eight grandchildren and six great-grandchildren and a lot of happiness and love because of them. They are easy to love—perfect—well, most of the time. For example, we have tried for two years to get a picture of me with four great-grandchildren, ages two, three, four, and eight, where we looked at least like we liked each other. Mission unaccomplished.

There have been a few failures. They're fun to be with,

but it's hard always to understand their language. I loved watching them climb on and fall off the round hay bales at the ranch, laughing and squealing all the time. I love them all so much. Grandchildren are one of God's greatest gifts, four-star!

P.S. Best of all, you can love 'em—spoil 'em—then send them home!

Denton Cooley

Denton Cooley is a world-renowned heart surgeon and founder of the Texas Heart Institute. His many honors include the Medal of Freedom, the nation's highest civilian award.

*A*fter having five daughters, it seemed that the message was clear enough that no sons were forthcoming for Louise and me. We resigned ourselves to wait for another generation. After four granddaughters arrived, the message was even clearer that no males were likely to arrive. Finally, the boys began to appear and of sixteen grandchildren, we have a perfect mixture of genders—eight and eight. They are all healthy—no heart ailments, for which I am grateful—and all thriving. Our grandchildren are a source of constant interest and pleasure for Louise and me after fifty-four years of marriage. Most of the sixteen are our close neighbors.

An incident occurred when my eldest grandson and namesake, Denton, was seventeen years old and junior golf champion at Houston Country Club. On Sunday morning, a life-long friend, Burt Magill, invited me to play golf with his family, including his twelve-year-old grandson Brett, an avid young golfer himself. Burt told his grandson that Dr. Cooley was going to join them. Brett's response was simply "OK." Burt then said, "Do you know who Dr. Cooley is?" "Yeah, I know who he is." Then Burt said, "OK, who is he?" With an off-hand gesture, Brett said, "He's Denton's granddaddy."

That is when I realized that any prospect of respect or hero worship was being transferred to my grandson who was a far better golfer than myself. Denton had become the hero, if any, to the younger generation.

Stephen Covey

Stephen B. Covey is the founder and chairman of the Covey Leadership Center and founder of The Institute for Principle-Centered Leadership. He is the author of The New York Times *bestseller,* The Seven Habits of Highly Effective People©.

THREE KEYS TO PARTNERING
WITH YOUR KIDS IN
RAISING YOUR GRANDCHILDREN

*T*hink about it for a moment. Think about whatever level of success you have achieved in life and answer this question: Is your success partly, or even largely, because someone believed in you when you didn't believe in yourself?

I frequently ask this question of large audiences and almost invariably half of the people raise their hands. If I ask them to share their stories, they not only come to tears, but so do many of their listeners.

To let your grandchild know that you really believe in him or her—that you're so proud of the person he or she is becoming—and of the tremendous potential they have, can be one of the most powerful and lasting influences you could ever have as a grandparent.

I watched my dear sister, Marilyn, die of a wasting cancer disease over a fairly long period of time. She had a large family with over twenty grandchildren. In her last few months she literally took every one-on-one opportunity she could find to communicate to each of her grandchildren their worth. The night before she passed, she gathered all of her children and grandchildren around her bed. It was a very crowded room. She took as little pain medicine as she could so that she would have as much access to her faculties as possible. She called each person in turn to her bedside to say goodbye and to affirm them one last time so that they would have the memory of their grandmother's love and belief in them. That was many years ago. Yet to this day, those children and grandchildren remember that night and are warmed by it. In fact, it seems to me that to a degree, most of them live on that and other such memories and that they hold them to a responsible course in life.

From time to time, I've learned to take a troubled grandchild and look him or her squarely in the eye in a private setting and just simply say, "You are not only my grandchild, you are a child of God. You have infinite worth. You have divine potential. You are not to compare yourself with anyone else. You are precious in your own right. I believe in you and love you with all my heart." I've often had a grandchild respond, "Would you please say that again?" I then attempted to develop some kind of special code name for them or a secret way of showing them love by hugging them or sharing an inside joke that he or she and I alone know, and it creates a very, very special bonding.

As parents of nine children and grandparents of forty-one, the three keys that my wife, Sandra, and I have found to really work are these:

I literally believe that the *first* and greatest thing you can do for your grandchildren is to affirm their parents, your own children, in the magnificent work they are doing. They are in the middle of the trenches, and some days, see nothing but problems and seeming failures. But we have found that, when we talk with them face-to-face, on the phone, and through correspondence, and simply affirm the great job they are doing—the courage that they are manifesting, the patience—often they respond with feelings of discouragement and failure over their lack of the very things that we are affirming in them—their overreactions, their impatience, etc. Even if they are making mistakes, remember, you are affirming their potential, their intention. It's the direction in which they're going. You affirm that which is not seen. That's what faith is: The evidence of things not seen.

When you affirm these deeper human capacities, it awakens their parental spirit within. It feeds their minds and their souls. They need it. They need it constantly, regularly. The more you continually affirm your own adult children, the more desire and capacity it gives them to affirm their children. It also establishes such a level of bonding partnership and genuine, authentic communication that they feel free to open up with their intimate fears, self-doubts, concerns and hopes. Intimate communication means "in-to-me-see." In this way, you become a light, rather than a judge. You become a model, rather than a critic. You become a source of emotional nurturance. And through this partnership, you literally can counsel each other back and forth without fear of stepping on toes or on emotional landmines. You can take directions from your children in how you can best help them raise their children. In doing so, you partner with your children and you can compensate for their weaknesses through your strengths. You can step in when they are low and provide your high.

The *second* great key to partnering with your kids in raising your grandchildren should perhaps be the first, because it is foundational to what has been already mentioned. It is to make an emotional commitment to be significantly involved in the lives of each of your grandchildren. Because of the *partnership* and authentic communication you enjoy, the commitment will be wise and in total harmony with the parents' desires.

I had dinner with a very prominent businessman who told me of his sad regret about never bonding with his children because of his consuming business interests. But then, all of a sudden, light came to his eyes as he pulled from under his chair a blueprint of a three-generation vacation home he was building on the beaches of Savannah, Georgia. He said, "I am trying to reach my own children through partnering with them in building this gathering place for our grandchildren. My children want the rebonding as much as I do, but the key is to have common purpose around the grandchildren."

I remember speaking to a very wealthy group of retirees living on one of the Florida Keys about the importance of the three-generation family. I was pointing out how joyful three-generation families are—how vital and significant grandparents are as role models, mentors, and affirmers on a constant basis to their grandchildren. We were all in a big luxurious hotel and their huge yachts were right outside.

They loved their grandchildren and, once or twice a year, would invite their grandchildren to join them for a glorious island and yacht vacation. Often, they would travel to be with their grandchildren on Christmas or Thanksgiving or other special holidays. But fundamentally, they were still relatively detached, uninvolved, safe and independent.

After the presentation, we discussed these issues and an authentic spirit enveloped the group. People began to express what was really happening in their families and how they felt about it. In most cases, they recognized that they were essentially detached—that they were, as one put it, "buying off" their grandchildren with things, vacations, presents, and pleasures—that they felt safe in retreating to their palatial estates and yachts without really sharing any of the responsibility and burden of being models and mentors to their grandchildren. Several openly expressed almost disgust with their lifestyle, of yachting and golfing and cocktailing and intellectualizing about life. They wanted to be closer, physically, so they could see them more often. They wanted more "in-to-me-see" communication with them. They wanted to be part of the more significant happenings in their grandchildren's lives—not just an occasional birthday or graduation. They really wanted to partner with their children in raising their grandchildren and knew that their grandchildren wanted it also.

I will never forget that experience or that feeling. I resolved then to stay very emotionally and physically present with each of my grandchildren—to do things with them regularly, to have special, private dates with them and to avoid the safe, detached, independent, retired lifestyle.

The *third* key to partnering with your kids in raising your grandchildren is to do long-range planning in establishing special traditions—traditions around special holidays, birthdays, vacations, one-on-one outings, joint educational experiences, and fun, entertaining, and educational family gatherings and reunions.

Every year, Sandra puts on one of our happiest family memories. All the grandchildren look forward to it—even the older ones—because they are involved in helping to pull it off. We all go to a special lake for a week or two in the summer and my wife, with the help of the older grandchildren, lays out a very exciting treasure hunt on what we call Bird Island. Family legend has it that pirates left their treasure on this island. The grandchildren have to follow the clue notes very carefully to find the treasure. Those who follow false clues or who are not careful in following instructions are thrown off course. The whole island is only about 200 yards long and 30 yards wide, so you can just envision all these grandkids looking everywhere they can. Sandra throws pennies and nickels and dimes in certain areas, which gets the kids to feel they are on the hot trail. Eventually, they dig up the hidden pirate treasure chest, which has a special present for each of the grandchildren with their name on it. Each present reflects my wife's knowledge of each grandchild's interests. One year, we had relatively little time, got busy and didn't hold the pirate's treasure hunt. We heard about it all through the winter and swore we would never miss it again. The kids absolutely love it. Even though it involves about two days of work on the part of my wife and many of the enlisted older grandchildren to prepare and organize everything, it is so unifying, fun, and memorable, and it is so worth it.

Anticipating a special event like this treasure hunt or a private one-on-one date is as exciting as the event itself, sometimes even more so. The anticipation can sometimes go on for weeks or months, particularly when the children are involved and when the special date or outing has their agenda in it. Every time you interact with them, you can talk about it and share your excitement. They can hardly wait! Their parents are thrilled, too, because it somewhat relieves them of that work and preparation and enables intergenerational bonding to take place.

Another important tradition is to have intergenerational family service projects. I know of one family that, on an annual basis, undertakes a significant service project for the homeless or some other group with special needs in one of the cities they live in. Some years they travel to a far-off country to help build houses for the poor or assist doctors in rehabilitation and facial surgeries. We are taught that to find one's life, one must lose it in the service of another. Similarly, for a family to become deep and anchored, it must be more than just about "me and mine"; it must be about "thee and thine," where there are special service projects that tap into the talents and special interests of the grandchildren. Can you imagine what an inspiring memory and model that provides? Such children will have their own families someday and will partner with their own kids to raise their grandkids.

Grandparents can become a very significant spiritual force inside a family that is buried in the thick of things. Grandparents have a larger perspective and often more wisdom. If they have the commitment, they can provide the kind of leadership that enables significant, memorable service projects to take place that serve other families and other special community needs.

Finally, let me suggest that you take pains to avoid five emotional cancers in your intergenerational families. These five are: criticizing, complaining, comparing, competing (for a sense of worth), and contending.

There is no one right way to be a grandparent. But I do believe that partnering with your children in raising your grandchildren is the right way. In fact, oftentimes, because of dysfunction, death, divorce, etc., grandparents must take over the role of parents and do so cheerfully, smilingly, knowing that fundamentally, life is a mission, not a career—that we all have a sacred stewardship for these special bundles from heaven.

Willard's Great Things to Do with Your Grandchildren

. . . . . .

Volunteer to teach your grandchildren how to ride a bike. Your children may enjoy the favor, and your grandchildren will remember this forever.

Take your grandchildren to your hometown, your old elementary school, your former camp. Show them the places that were special to you during your childhood.

Read to *your* grandchildren from *your* favorite book. If you no longer have it, you can probably find it at a library or at some used bookseller online.

Write a family song together.

Take them to an amusement park. Children of all ages love amusement parks.

Let them dictate a story to you. It can be about anything. Type the story and present it to your grandchildren as a present.

Go on a picnic.

. . . . . .

Perfect love sometimes does not come until grandchildren are born.

—WELSH PROVERB

Walter Cunningham

Walter Cunningham is an astronaut who successfully piloted the Apollo VII spacecraft on an eleven-day voyage. He is known as NASA's "second civilian astronaut."

THERE IS NOT AN INCH OF HER THAT DOESN'T MAKE MY HEART LEAP

*A*s I write about my feelings for grandchildren, I realize I have been blessed with six of the sweetest and most capable grandchildren on the face of the earth. Of course, most grandparents feel that way about their grandchildren. In this case, it's the absolute truth.

Flying with the Marine Corps and attending graduate school, while working sometimes five jobs, followed by eight years as a NASA astronaut, interfered with my being the father I would like to have been when my children were young. I was there for them, but the frantic pace left little time for parenting for the first ten years of their lives. So I don't want to miss any time with my grandchildren.

Each of the six is very special and loving in their own way and I could write a poem about each. However, I will share my feelings about my first grandchild, because she made me realize and appreciate the awesome responsibility of being a grandparent.

Butterflies, cotton candy, pink bubble gum, stickers, hugs and kisses—every moment with Jessica fills me with wonder and happiness and admiration. Being such a joy, I hold close to my heart every giggle, every laugh, and every needy cry. Every time she reaches up and takes my hand to walk beside me, it is better than an afterburner kicking in on the latest fighter plane.

It is a godsend to watch her grow, to see her first tooth, watch her first steps, say her first word, make a half sentence, develop a sweet personality, and show signs of brilliance. And yes, like all little ones, she can occasionally be a little defiant or even smart-mouthed.

My heart takes leave when she cuddles up close after

dinner with a bowl of ice cream and we settle in to watch a television show or her favorite video. She wedges in between my body and the arm of the chair, puts her arm around me, and throws her legs across mine. She will cover her mouth and whisper in my ear, sharing secrets I promise never to tell. As she gets sleepy, she will cuddle just a little more and whisper, "I love you, Papa," before dropping off to sleep. Jessica's sweet love is like angel dust sprinkling down from heaven and filling your soul and every pore of your body, making you feel content.

There was the time when Jessica was six and diving off the board into the deep end of the pool. She urged four-year-old Travis to take the jump, like she was doing. Fearless little Travis, bless his heart, made sure I was watching and jumped right in. When it was plain he was spending more time under the water than swimming to the side, I jumped in and pulled him to the surface. No sooner had Travis reached the top than he said, "Thank you, Papa, for saving me." He turned to his sister and said, "I told you I could do it."

I have known precious little fear in my own life, facing each challenge head-on. Yet, I fear that my grandchildren are not cautious enough to be protected from harm. I leap for joy at the opportunities that lie before them, but Jessica is so innocent and trusting, my inclination is to put her away like a precious heirloom. What is life if not to be lived? I know that answer as well as anyone. I've been blessed with more challenge and adventure than I could have imagined, and it came through having a good education and being prepared. I try hard to instill in my grandchildren an appreciation for the rewards of a quality education.

As a grandparent, there are a few things that I emphasize to Jessica and others of her age, because I feel they need to hear them. Lessons from grandparents are more lasting, even though the children may not seem to be listening. Dedication and commitment to yourself, your family, your community, your country, and to your life's goals are not to be taken lightly. It will ensure you become your own person and will define the path you are to travel.

You can be either a leader or a follower. A leader chooses his own direction and pace and others are attracted to follow him. A follower is merely one of the pack, doing what his "friends" do with little regard for how it will affect his life.

I was one of the fortunate few to have enjoyed a special experience, but it came about through dedicated, hard work, long nights of study, and short- and long-term goal planning, while sometimes working five jobs to support a family. I was ready—physically, mentally, and education- and health-wise—when the opportunity to become an astronaut presented itself. I wish I could get each grandchild in America to realize how much more important sacrifice is for success than surrendering to peer pressure and living for today. Living just for today can not only get you into big trouble but it can strip you of the opportunities and valuable rewards that life has to offer.

We lead such full and busy lives trying to "make it," that we frequently forget how to show our emotions. That is a circumstance I wanted to avoid with my grandchildren. It feels wonderful to say, "I love you, Honey," and know that they know I really mean it. I want with all my heart for them to know that Papa will always be there for them.

The wonderful memory of each development and event in Jessica's life is as fresh today as it was when they occurred: playing with Papa's cowboy boots was such a treat for her. She would struggle to get her shoes and socks off and slip into my closet and when she came out, she'd be standing in my big, brown cowboy boots. She would fall each time she tried to walk, then giggle, and look up for approval that it was okay. The rest of us, of course, were laughing with her.

Or, at the launch of a space shuttle, sitting on my lap as we watched the rocket burn its way into space, trailing a blazing streak of orange and red. "Papa! You did that, too, didn't you?" Jessica asked with as much wonder as excitement. She had to have verification from me and I was delighted to give it to her with a hug.

Whatever else my accomplishments in life, I most want to be known as a caring and loving Papa.

> By the time the youngest children have learned to keep the house tidy, the oldest grandchildren are on hand to tear it to pieces.
>
> —CHRISTOPHER MORLEY

Doug Daft

Doug Daft is chairman of the Board of Directors and CEO of The Coca-Cola Company, a Fortune 100 company. He has held a variety of leadership positions within the company since 1969.

A few years ago, I was named chairman of the Board of Directors and chief executive officer of The Coca-Cola Company. It has been the greatest honor of my professional life. But it does not begin to compare to James.

James is the son of my daughter, Alexandra. He is the nephew of—and a principal source of fun for—my son, Nick. For my wife, Delphine, and me, James is a lunch companion, a nap partner and, when we babysit, the most important customer we've ever entertained. He is, in short, the nearest thing to joy I can imagine.

James takes me out of managerial mode more swiftly and completely than any other personal activity. Perhaps the passage of time has helped me recognize more with him than with Nick or Alexandra that a stroll through the woods can be an enormously exciting adventure for a child. James' wonder and excitement in seeing an insect, a bird, or a flower rekindles a familiar excitement and appreciation of nature that has sometimes been crowded out of my consciousness in my busy years of career-building.

Robert Woodruff, the legendary former leader of The Coca-Cola Company, regularly reminded his colleagues that, "The world belongs to the discontented." And in today's hypercompetitive marketplace, the manager who does not commit himself or herself to continuous improvement will not stay in business—let alone succeed—for long.

And that may be why, for many business leaders I know, grandchildren are the ultimate reward. For Delphine and me, James is a source of complete, total contentment. And even though we think he's already perfect, he is the living embodiment of continuous improvement—every day with James is better than the day before.

I would enthusiastically recommend to any friend or colleague the wonderful sport of grandparenting. It can be as simple or as elaborate as you care to make it. It can involve physical or mental games. But in the final analysis, it is an activity of the heart.

David Dale

David Dale is a poet whose works include What We Call Our Own, Montana Primer, *and* Stumbling Over Stones.

THE WAY A BEAR IS

For Derrick Logan Dale

*Derrick stomps. "That's about
how hard the ground gets
when bears are walking, Grandpa."*

*The dust settles—
on my fishing hat
and in the patch of mutilated bushes,*

*their chokecherry stripped.
"Grandpa, look. Here's his poop."
Derrick pokes the berries*

*with his stick counting
as far as he knows in Spanish.
—"Once, trece, doce."*

This order doesn't phase
the old teacher, engaged,
with the indentation of a boulder

flipped aside for mealybugs.
"That rock's a landmark, Grandpa,
and here's my hatchet cut

"on this pine tree. It points
to the spot I fished with Dad last year."
We fight our way

down through the nettles, wild roses
and . . . "Look out, Grandpa!
That's poisoned ivy—"

to the backwater swamp.
I spar with cattails and Russian
thistles, falling twice.

"Here, Grandpa, take my stick."
Ahh, the river—but in the riffles
just below the hole, the bear,

a Grizzly playing with a Rainbow
flopping on the bank. He looks up—
"Oh, my God, he'll see us . . ."

"Shhh! Walk real quiet, Grandpa,
We'll hide inside these aspen trees
and let him fish the hole."

Charlie Daniels

Charlie Daniels has been a professional musician for more than five decades, spanning the various genres of rock & roll, bluegrass, and country. His numerous hits include such legendary songs as "The Devil Went Down to Georgia" and "Long Haired Country Boy." He recently released his autobiography, Ain't No Rag: Freedom, Family, and the Flag.

I am firmly convinced that the greatest gift God ever gave to mankind is children of our own. Children bring a sweetness to our lives that nothing else can provide. And if children are the dessert of life, grandchildren are the icing.

"Mom, you never let me jump up and down on the furniture like that." "Why in the world did you buy that for him? His room is so full of toys now that you can't walk in it." "You've already taken him to Disney World once this year."

Well, so what? Grandchildren are the most privileged characters on the planet. Who else can have breakfast at the Pancake House, lunch at McDonald's, and dinner at Chuck E. Cheese's?

Evan has more vehicles in our garage than we do, not to mention two sets of golf clubs, a horse, a swing set, and his own little snowmobile in Colorado. The phrase, "Evan is spending the night," starts a flurry of activity at our house as Hazel checks the supply of gooey cereal and ice cream.

So just what is it about these munchkins that melts the hearts of aging people, these miniature tyrants with the chocolate milk mustaches? I'm sure I can't answer that to everyone's satisfaction, but to me it's a lot of things. It's the innocent eyes not yet clouded by worldly cares and the absolute trust that only a small child can have. It's the joy of watching them tear open brightly colored packages at Christmas time. It's the thrill of being there for the first fish he catches or teaching him how to hold a golf club or shoot a .22 rifle. It's taking him on his first plane flight. It's hugs and kisses and deep feelings that only our grandson could foster.

It's just plain wonderful. God bless all the grandchildren.

❧　❧

Jack Davis

Jack Davis is a cartoonist who worked on a variety of titles in the 1950s, including Two-Fisted Tales *and* Mad *magazine. Davis has since branched out into illustration for advertising; he has illustrated album covers for musicians and magazine covers for* Time *magazine.*

Her grandchildren were bringing new joy to her life, a joy that illuminated her face whenever you saw them together. Whether it was taking Rose and Tatiana for an ice cream cone, or taking a walk in Central Park with little Jack as she did last Sunday, she relished being Grand Jackie and showering her grandchildren with love.

—SENATOR EDWARD KENNEDY ON
JACQUELINE KENNEDY ONASSIS

Alan Dershowitz

Alan M. Dershowitz is a professor of law at Harvard Law School and an author. His latest book is The Case for Israel.

*I*t was dinnertime and I turned to one of my dinner companions and said, "I'd like to talk to you for a few minutes." He responded, "I'm sorry, but you're too boring to talk to. I just wanna eat." The other dinner companion objected, "You shouldn't talk to him that way," to which the first responded, "But he *is* boring." The second said, "That's true, but you still shouldn't say it." Normally, I would walk away from the table in a huff. But the first dinner companion was my eight-year-old grandson speaking truth to power. The second was my ten-year-old grand-daughter trying to teach her younger brother some manners. I've been called many things in my life, but never before was I called boring. But to my eight-year-old grandson, having a discussion about school with his grandpa is the epitome of boredom. Of course, being a lawyer who's learned how to think on his feet, I immediately switched the subject to the latest Daredevil and Spiderman movies. Suddenly I was no longer boring—not by any means fascinating mind you, but at least I had crossed the threshold beyond utter boredom.

I have two grandchildren, Lyle who is eight and Laurie who is ten. It's hard to believe that two human beings with identical genetic backgrounds could be so different. Laurie is intense, serious, ambitious. She reads voraciously, but keeps most of her ideas to herself. Lyle is what my grandmother would have called a "trumbanick." I have no idea of the etymology of that exotic-sounding word, but I can tell you what it connotes: a troublemaker with a constant gleam in his eye and an inability to censor his thoughts. Of course, they are both brilliant and gorgeous. Everyone's grandchild is.

I am in the unusual position of having a daughter only three years older than my granddaughter. They are very similar in many ways and are great friends. Because they are so close in age and so similar, they constitute the perfect control experiment as to the difference between being a father and a grandfather. The relationship between child and grandchild is very different. I, along with my wife, am responsible for my daughter in so many ways—her education, her healthcare, her religious upbringing. I am not responsible for my grandchildren in the same way. I may have a vote, but certainly not a veto. And my vote is often ignored, as well it should be. Though I have no direct responsibility for my grandchildren, I care deeply about every aspect of their lives. I speak to them just about every day. Sometimes we have serious discussions, more often it is just catching up or giving a little encouragement. I am absolutely certain that I get much more out of these discussions than they do, but that's one of my rights as a grandfather—to bore my grandchildren.

My son, who is a real wise guy, decided to name me "Poppa Al" for my grandchildren. He knows full well that I despise "Al" since I have told him many times that the only people who call me Al are people I don't get along with. So he figured he'd neutralize the name by including it in my official grandfather title. In the beginning I had trouble getting used to it, because it sounded like a pizza shop. But I hear it so often now that it has become a natural part of my relationship with my grandkids. (If you're not one of my grandchildren, don't even try to call me "Al.")

I work hard trying not to be boring to my grandchildren. I know that I am only partly successful, but it's a work in progress. And it's the greatest and most enjoyable challenge in the world.

A good man leaveth an inheritance to his children's children.

—PROVERBS 13:22

Ann Deschanel

Ann Deschanel is the grandmother of Zooey Deschanel, a musician and actress. Ann is a proud grandmother of four and currently lives in Colorado.

I have always lived 1,800 miles away from Zooey. Our associations were slim and infrequent. One event that I remember is the recognition of Zooey's singing voice. I was visiting her family when Zooey was eight and was awakened by an incredible voice. "Was it an opera recording?" I asked myself. No, it was Zooey, engaged in a voice lesson. At a young age, she had quite an enormous voice. She now sings at the Roosevelt Hotel in Los Angeles. Zooey's great-grandfather was in the Metropolitan Chorus, and the entire family has a history of choral singing. Zooey got her voice honestly!

Phyllis Diller

Phyllis Diller is a comedienne known for her candid wit and outrageous style.

I have four grandsons and when I think of what fun granddaughters could have had with my wardrobe and wigs, I think, what a waste!

Phil Donahue

Phil Donahue is a legendary television personality. His show, Donahue, *aimed at "women who think," brought about a new, more modern era in daytime entertainment.*

I literally cannot take my eyes off my grandchildren. When they both sit on my lap (ages five and seven), I am at peace and filled with a joy I have never known.

Then the war breaks out!

I am on the front lines. I am a mediator; I hand out candy; I make funny noises with my vibrating lips (my best trick). When the conflict subsides, I escort them back to the Parental Command Post. And then I go to bed and sleep like a baby.

Archie Dunham

Archie W. Dunham is the chairman of the board of Cono-coPhillips, Inc., one of the world's leading integrated petroleum companies. Among his many honors, Mr. Dunham was presented the Horatio Alger Award in 2001 and was named a "Legend of Industry" by the A&D Summit in 2002.

IT'S ONE OF LIFE'S GREATEST BLESSINGS TO BE A GRANDPARENT

*I*n a society where everyone is moving at the speed of light, grandchildren slow us down, allowing parents and grandparents a respite from our treadmill existence. The quick smile of a four-year-old grandson jumping into your lap, the loving hug and kiss of a granddaughter, or a serious conversation, golf, or chess match with a maturing grandson can make even the busiest company chairman or CEO stop and enjoy the moment.

Childhood is a time of constant and dramatic change. The presence of grandparents in children's lives has a reassuring effect; they provide stability, continuity, and, hopefully, role models for parenting, happiness, and success. Grandparents are living links to the past, even as they encourage their grandchildren to dream of the future. Grandparents influence their grandchildren directly, but also exert an indirect influence, by virtue of having raised their grandchildren's parents. In innumerable obvious and subtle ways, grandparents help children forge their identities and their destinies.

I'll always remember the birth of our first grandchild. My wife, Linda, and I were vacationing in Hawaii with some of the friends we had made there while I was serving in the United States Marine Corps. We knew that our oldest son and his wife were expecting their first child, so it was a time of great anxiety and thrilling expectation for everyone. One day, I was trying to ease the strain of waiting by playing golf with old friends. When we returned to the hotel, I found that Linda had fashioned streamers from toilet paper proclaiming, "It's a boy . . . it's a boy," and hung them on the door of our hotel room. We were grandparents. That was one of the happiest moments of my life!

CEOs of large corporations are powerful chieftains, but they take direction from even their youngest grandchildren. I'll always remember one of my granddaughters telling me that "I was in real 'crouble,'" because I wasn't doing a good job of playing "dolls" with her. I left her room determined to "get it right" next time!

Several years ago our family (all sixteen of us) started a tradition of family vacations. Participation was voluntary. Granddad picked up the bill, but the only obligation was for everybody to have fun . . . grandparents, parents, and grandchildren. Since then we've taken vacations to Africa and watched wildlife from a hot air balloon at sunrise; we've snorkeled in Hawaii; we've captured whales in a camera lens in Alaska; and we've ridden horses on a dude ranch in Colorado. We've also eaten ice cream at Disney World and played with Donald Duck on a Disney cruise to the Bahamas, to name just a few of our destinations. We worried at first if the parents would revert to children, or if our grandkids would argue and fight. Instead, we've enjoyed these unique opportunities to be together and observe the wonders of God's creation. Our children have enjoyed being with each other and our grandkids have loved being with their cousins. It's been a wonderful experience that we renew every year.

One of the wisest decisions Linda and I have made over the years is to treat each of our grandchildren to their "trip of a lifetime" when they reach age sixteen. The custom originated with a promise to our oldest granddaughter that we would take her to Paris, France, or anywhere in the world she wanted to see, when she became sixteen. The other grandchildren were quick to demand equal treatment.

Our two oldest grandsons, who are cousins, elected to take their trip together, with Antarctica as the destination. The adventure began last December, and lasted through the Christmas holidays and New Year's, ending in January 2003. We traveled from California and Texas to Argentina, then across Drake's Passage to the barren, frigid, and magnificent continent of Antarctica. We enjoyed long dinners together, played games until granddad was ready for bed, marveled at the beautiful blue icebergs at sunset, observed millions of penguins sliding down the icy slopes on their bellies, and were mesmerized by the jagged snow-covered mountains. It was a wonderful experience that grandmother and granddaddy will never forget. We cannot wait for the next six trips! The writer Alex Haley once said, "Nobody can do for little children what grandparents do. Grandparents sort of sprinkle stardust over the lives of little children." Hopefully, Linda and I are doing that with our eight wonderful grandchildren: Christopher, David, Sarah, Eric, Ashley, Sydney, Chandler, and Bryce. We love them all, and their wonderful parents!

The baby is not yet born, and yet you say that his nose is like his grandfather's.

—INDIAN PROVERB

Hy Eisman

Hy Eisman is a cartoonist and comic book artist. His work includes the classic comic strips Blondie, Nancy, The Katzenjammer Kids, *and the Sunday* Popeye *strip.*

"SOMETHING I NEVER LET MY OWN CHILDREN DO..."

Willard's Favorite Nicknames for Grandparents

. . . . . .

Amma	Mawmaw
Big Dad	Nanna
Gammy	Nanny
Grammy	Nini
Gramp	Poppie
Gramps	Pop Pop
Grandma	Poppy
Grandpa	

Michael Enzi

Michael B. Enzi took office as a senator from Wyoming in 1997. He has brought his knowledge of accounting to the Senate, as a ranking member of the Securities and Investments Subcommittee and a member of the Committee on the Budget.

The text that follows is a floor speech that Senator Enzi gave about his new grandson on September 16, 2003.

*M*r. President, this last weekend I got a new name. Fifty-nine years ago, when I was born, I was named Michael Bradley Enzi. The middle name comes from my Grampa and Gramma Bradley on my mother's side. They were homesteaders in Montana. My grandfather on my dad's side homesteaded in North Dakota and named his son Elmer, but he died shortly after I was born and before I could know him. My dad's favorite song was "Elmer's Tune," but he thought there were enough Elmers already and named me Michael. I grew up being Mickey and then Mike. As I mentioned, this last weekend I got a new name and I am truly delighted.

I am now Grampa—and that is spelled with an 'M,'

not an 'N,' and there is no 'D' in it. I will explain that in just a moment.

My son and his wife had a son. My son, also like me, had the good fortune to overmarry, to Danielle, a delightful young lady from Kentucky whom he met in Washington, D.C. She is one of the most organized, focused, and thoughtful people I know. My son Brad and daughter-in-law Danielle had a son. I cannot begin to share the emotion and feeling that overwhelms me today. It is such an incredible feeling to hold another generation in your hands.

When my son was born, we named him Michael Bradley Enzi, as well, and instead of giving him the title "Junior," we just used his middle name, Brad, to avoid confusion. Now we have a third Michael Bradley Enzi, but we do not believe in titles so we call him Trey to avoid confusion. Now Danielle and Trey had extremely fortunate timing for Diana and me. Trey was supposed to be born the end of this month, but he and his mother moved that up to when Diana and I were in the neighborhood. Diana and I met Brad and Danielle on Friday so I could get the "transportation system." We used to call those "strollers and car seats"; now it is "transportation systems." My dad started the tradition of buying wheels for my kids.

That means the wagons, the skateboards, the rollerblades, the bikes, et cetera. When I heard I was going to be a grampa, I staked the "wheels" out, too.

So we picked out the transportation system. Danielle thought she started having contractions. We knew she had walked a lot, so Brad checked her into the hospital at midnight. At 8 A.M., the water broke, and at 4:21 P.M., Saturday, September 13, we all got new names. Trey weighed six pounds, fourteen ounces and was twenty and a half inches long, with huge hands and long feet. Of course, his six-foot eight-inch dad—who played basketball for Wyoming—has size sixteen feet and easily palms a basketball.

Danielle came through, as is her nature, invigorated and enthusiastic. You would not have known by looking at her face, except for that special aura of being a mother, that she had just given birth. The rest of us were emotional wrecks. The best way I can tell you of the thrill is to tell you that we canceled the events of the weekend and extended an extra day, and I spent as much of that time as I could just holding that baby, watching him breathe and move ever so slightly, and listened to every little sound he made. Of course, I had to let Diana hold him a little, too. And his mom and dad even wanted turns!

If you would have told me I would spend hours just gazing at this miracle of life, and having only that thought for hours, I probably wouldn't have believed you. But I have some instant replay memories of that little face and those moving hands and those blankets and that cap, to hold the body heat in, locked in my mind.

I am constantly doing little instant replay memories for myself and thanking God for the opportunities he has given me—from finding Diana and learning about prayer with our first child, the daughter who was born premature, who showed us how worthwhile fighting for life is, to the birth of our son, to the birth of our youngest daughter, who just got married, to helping me through open heart surgery so that I might have this chance to hold yet another generation in my hands.

I think of the Prayer of Jabez in Chronicles, where he says: "Lord, please continue to bless me, indeed." And to that I add my thanks for this and all the blessings noticed and unnoticed.

So I am a grampa. That is not grandfather—too stilted. Years ago, my daughter gave me a hand-stitched wall hanging that says: "Any man can be a Father, but it takes someone special to be a Dad."

The name is also not grandpa. This is a little too elevated. My Grampa—spelled with an 'M' and no 'D'—my Grampa Bradley took me on some wonderful adventures. He taught me a lot—fishing, hunting, and work. He "let" me help him plant and water trees when I was four. He showed me how to chop sagebrush and make flagstone walks. He covered up holes he encouraged me to dig. He covered them so people wouldn't drive a car into them. He taught me how to spade a garden, mow a lawn, and trim it properly.

He later showed me the point in life when you are supposed to start carrying the heavy end of the log. Later in life, he had heart trouble and couldn't go fishing by himself, so he took me along. After a few minutes, he would place himself at the picnic area and visit with the tourists who stopped. He would tell then about his grandson who would be arriving shortly with fish and have quite a group waiting for my return.

He liked to be called Grampa. And I am now delighted to have the opportunity to earn that name. I wish I could adequately share with you the joy in my heart.

Trey, grandson, welcome to this world of promise and hope and love.

I yield the floor.

Thy pardon, Father, I beseech,
In this my prayer if I offend;
One something sees beyond his reach
From childhood to his journey's end.
My wife, our little boy Aignan,
Have travelled even to Narbonne;
My grandchild has seen Perpignan;
And I—have not seen Carcassonne.

—GUSTAVE NADAUD

Anne Francis

Anne Francis was a child model, beginning her career at the young age of five and appearing in more than 3,000 radio spots before she was ten. She received a Golden Globe Award for her performance as Honey West in the hit television series of the same name and went on to appear in several films.

BRIAN

I first saw his beautiful profile two months before he was born, when my daughter, Jane, was visiting me in Santa Barbara and showed us his sonogram picture at her baby shower. Adorable! Sweet innocence resting in the womb of his mom. My next meeting was two days after his birth, when I flew to Colorado Springs to meet this new visitor to Earth, now named Brian. He had the quiet stare that his mom had had when I first met her face-to-face! Two months before Jane was born, she leaped in my womb when thunder pealed over our home in Westwood. I laughed with surprise, and immediately she settled down, confirming my belief that babes could hear all that was happening around their mother as they matured in the womb. Doctors in those days disclaimed that sort of thing, but we mothers knew what was what. We didn't have a clue in those days what the sex of the child would be, but because Jane seemed to be pole-vaulting a great deal of the time, it was assumed "It" would be a boy! I was rooting for a girl, because, in the first place, I didn't know much about children, having lived and worked in an adult world since I was six, and second, I really didn't know anything at all about little boys!

Well, now I have my little boy, and what a treat he is! He has remained so since the first moment when he nestled on my chest as I sang "Daisy, Daisy, Give Me Your Answer Do," to a recent visit when they flew in to see me, and Brian and I swung in the garden swing and discussed the frog that had just jumped out of the watering can and the funny seed pods that the giant jacarandas hovering over us would soon be dropping. I promised I would send him a box of those pods that looked like little cartoon faces with big, open beaklike mouths. I have been meaning to decorate some for years, and now that Brian is here, I know he would not think me strange for doing so. I think that is what I love the most about him. He will join in with my playful nature. "Gramma is funny!" he'll say. Music to my ears. I just love to hear him laugh.

Soon he will be three, and he will start on the road of pre-school, and kindergarten, and then up the ladder of conventional "learning." And he will hear about all kinds of scary things, but also wonderful things as well, and I pray that I will be here when he grows up into the studious, dark-eyed young man I know he will be. I also pray

I will still be able to get him to laugh now and then in this bewildering world he will inhabit for whatever his "hitch" may be.

As grandparents, our role is "Love 'em, and leave 'em." Perhaps because we are so acutely aware of that fact, we hope we can leave them with a chuckle in their heart after we have gone. Some warm times they can remember when Life gets a bit too cold, as it has a way of doing. I was blessed to have been here to greet Brian, and if all goes well, I pray I may greet him once more in the far distant future when his time on this planet is through. Whenever and wherever that may be, that's a date I plan to keep!

A grandmother is a babysitter who watches the kids instead of the television.

—ANONYMOUS

Bill Gallo

Bill Gallo is a sportswriter who writes primarily about boxing. He has received accolades from the Boxing Writers Association of America for his columns about the sport, and in 2001 he was inducted into the International Boxing Hall of Fame for his work as a journalist.

I am the grandfather of Stephanie, age twenty-six, and Amy, age twenty-two. They are gifts from my oldest son, Gregory, and his wife, Deborah. Then stepping down the ladder are Marianna, age eleven, and Isabella, age eight. And this gift to us is from our youngest son, Bill, and his wife, K.T. I use the word gift, because without getting sappy, the four mentioned are the loveliest of presents given to me and my wife.

It's a wonderful thing to hold each one of them as infants and it gets better watching them grow. Every one is a different individual with their own special talents. They tickle the heart. I suppose most grandparents feel the same way, but I don't know if they express it. They should, though, because it's such an easy thing to do. All it takes is being around them, unlocking your heart, and just saying what's in there. That simple, honest joy they bring.

Four girls and would we trade them for boys? No sir, these are keepers.

The first set of granddaughters calls us "Gramp" and "Grandma." The second settled for "Poppy and Mimi." In both cases it was their own choice.

To my readers, I'm Bill Gallo, columnist and cartoonist for the New York *Daily News*, and I like being that, since I've loved being a newspaper man all my life, but for some years now, the names I like even better are "Gramps and Poppie." Is having grandchildren the best fun any person can have? Absolutely. If there were just one reason for me to be pictured on Willard's 100 + Smucker's label, it would be to see all four granddaughters happy with their lives.

Art Ginsburg

Art Ginsburg revolutionized the television chef persona by of-
fering recipes that were good to eat, easy to follow, and quick
to prepare. Fans around the world watch his syndicated show,
Mr. Food, *every day.* Mr. Food *has also written over thirty*
best-selling cookbooks, including cookbooks written in con-
junction with the American Diabetes Association.

I have to admit it—I wasn't around a heck of a lot when
my kids were little. During the day I was working hard at a
series of less than successful business ventures, while
many an evening was spent either involved in community
service work or pursuing my true passion—performing.

Honing my acting skills, raising three kids, and building a catering business with my wife, Ethel, kept our lives
pretty full. It took many years and lots of determination to
develop the *Mr. Food* show out of my love of performing
and my love of food. All that work didn't leave a lot of
time for me to nurture my three children. Fortunately,
Ethel made up for my shortcomings in that area! And, fortunately for us both, our kids could be with us when we
were catering parties every weekend—working beside us,
gaining a great work ethic and solid values along the way.

Sure, our kids knew that, as busy as we were, we were always there for them. We somehow always made it to their ball games, band concerts, and such, and we made time for regular family outings every summer—drive-in movies (with the kids in their pj's, spread out in the back of the station wagon), camping in the Adirondack Mountains, and, later, an annual summer vacation at the seashore. These family excursions weren't fancy by any means, but they were oh, so sweet, and that's probably why they're my favorite memories of time spent with my kids.

Of course, there were tough, harrowing times between then and now—including all the nights we waited up for them to come home from being out with friends (there were no cell phones in those days!), and dropping off our only daughter, Caryl, at her first apartment in New York City when she moved there right after college.

Well, Steve, Caryl, and Chuck are grown now, with children of their own. They've made Ethel and me grandparents six times over! No matter how much our friends told us how wonderful it is to be grandparents (and they told us often!), we couldn't have known the feelings it would bring out in us until we had our own grandchildren. And as busy as I've been since the oldest, Shayna, was born thirteen years ago, I've somehow managed to be around to enjoy and appreciate special times with each of them.

Shayna, Jessie, Beth, Sam, Alyssa, and Noa are the lights of my life, and I love being there when they receive school and community service awards as much as I love simply watching them eat their breakfast after spending the night with Grandma Ethel and me, or playing on the beach with each other.

Being with my grandchildren gives me strength, and also satisfaction. I may not have been able to spend as much time as I would have liked with my own kids in their early years, but watching their children grow and develop into confident, bright, and happy young adults gives me a feeling of completion. Ethel and I must have done a pretty good job, because our children, along with their loving and generous spouses, have given us, and the world, six amazing individuals.

My kids are great, but the relationship of parents and children is so close that you know all too well how to push each other's buttons. With grandchildren, everything's different. Practically everything they say is a jewel, and things that would have really driven me crazy if my own kids had done them are so darned cute when it comes to my grandchildren! I guess it proves how much I've mellowed over the years.

Grandchildren are so easy to love—they're a joy. Gee, I wish I had twelve more . . . *first!*

—"Pop Pop" Art Ginsburg, a.k.a. Mr. Food

❧ ❧

Monty Hall

Monty Hall co-created and hosted the hit television game show Let's Make a Deal. *His charitable and philanthropic work has been recognized with many honors, including the Order of Canada and the Variety Clubs International Humanitarian Award.*

*H*aving five grandchildren, ages twenty-four to two, my wife, Marilyn, and I have never been without little ones, and, may I add, never been without the greatest joy and happiness that grandchildren bring. We are blessed with five and are thankful, but sometimes I wish we had a dozen, because each one in his or her own way adds a special rose to life's bouquet.

If you would civilize a man, begin with his grand-mother.

—VICTOR HUGO

Charles Harmon

Charles B. Harmon is a former major league baseball player who broke the Cincinnati Reds' color barrier in 1954 when he became their first African-American player. He went on to play for the St. Louis Cardinals, the Philadelphia Phillies, and the winter leagues in Puerto Rico.

THE JOY THAT GRANDCHILDREN BRING TO MIND DURING ONE'S LIFETIME

* The birth of our granddaughter.
* The birth of our grandson.
* Creating an everlasting legacy of ourselves to mankind.
* The rejuvenation of ourselves after our own children have grown and left the nest and then their children return.
* The joy you get when they visit with you and the relief you receive after they go home.
* A remarkable chance to correct the mistakes we think we may have made with our own children.
* The added excitement at special celebrations and holidays with our grandchildren—Christmas, Thanksgiving, vacation, birthdays, etc.

- The ability to truly enjoy when our grandchildren cut or lose their first tooth, the first time they crawl, their first step, their first word, or when they say mama, papa, grandma, grandpa.
- Their first day at school, their graduation, their wedding.
- Turning sixteen—getting their driving permit or their license.
- Their first official date.
- Being a retired major league baseball player and taking my grandchildren to the ball games during spring training in Florida and to the Great American Ball Park. Also, taking them to visit the players on the field and on tours of all the clubhouses.
- Playing catch with my grandson.

Derek Hathaway

Derek C. Hathaway is the chairman, president, and CEO of Harsco Corporation, a market leader in several global industries, including steel, construction, gas, and energy.

One of the first real sentences uttered by our granddaughter sitting on my knee was, "I wub you, Papa," which I interpreted to mean, "I love you, Papa." I dissolved into tears, and responded "I wub you too, Sophie."

Shortly after that event, I was in a business meeting with my immediate colleagues. The atmosphere was, as usual, professional, and the meeting lengthy. During a brief break, knowing of my previously stated joy and enthusiasm for our grandparental status, a colleague inquired as to how things were with our new little granddaughter. My demeanor must have brightened instantly and I responded by reciting the aforementioned incident, mimicking the appropriate baby language. The meeting reconvened and I returned to my CEO role. At the close, the colleague who had originally inquired made the observation that if they were given a choice, my colleagues infinitely preferred to deal with the gentler and kinder "Papa" rather than the chairman and CEO.

I was touched by his humor and keen observation about the many roles we are called upon to play in our lives, and for me nothing compares to the experience of love and affection in a close and supportive family environment.

Marilyn Horne

Marilyn Horne is a concert and opera singer. She founded the Marilyn Horne Foundation to encourage and preserve the art of the vocal recital.

When Daisy was born (October 17, 1998), I said, "I never knew that I could love anyone this much in my lifetime." And then when Henry was born (January 17, 2003), I said the same thing all over again. Now I feel that my cup truly runneth over.

If you know his father and grandfather, don't worry about his son.

—AFRICAN PROVERB

Jon Huntsman

Jon M. Huntsman is the founder and CEO of Huntsman Corporation, an international chemical company, and is also known for his philanthropic endeavors, including the development of the Huntsman Cancer Foundation in 1995. He is currently Deputy U.S. Trade Representative with the rank of Ambassador.

I now have fifty grandchildren, and my favorite sport is to hang out with them. They are the best! No other activity could compensate for romping with your grandchildren—

except tuning into Willard and getting the latest weather report.

Sybil Jason

Sybil Jason began her career in show business as a child star on the Warner Brothers sets in the late 1930s. She made her screen debut in Little Big Shot *in 1935.*

*H*ow does one define the word grandparent, that can encompass so many emotions . . . so much love . . . so much pride . . . so much of everything that is good.

Personally, the closest that I can come is the feeling that I had after giving birth to my daughter Toni. A similar feeling returned almost sixteen years ago when my grandson Daniel was born. On that important occasion, I instantly recognized that familiar feeling that was now an extension and a continuation of the unconditional love one human being gladly bestows upon another . . . mother to daughter . . . grandmother to grandson.

One of the many delightful things about observing one's grandchild is seeing the world through his unjaded eyes. Everything is new and fresh and exciting, and his obvious thrill at each new discovery in turn gives the grandparent the opportunity to relive the enthusiasms of her own youth. That is the priceless gift that the younger generation gives to the older one.

I am often asked by couples who have not become grandparents yet whether there is a downside to it.

Well, perhaps there are brief moments when our pride and joy go through the terrible twos or the confusion of puberty and when that happens, and I smile as I write this, we temporarily release our grandparenting skills and gently and gratefully return them to the sanctity of their own homes and let their parents deal with it!

Ah yes, there are many joys attached to this business of grandparenting and wisely, this is one of them!

Take care and watch yourselves closely, so as neither to forget the things that your eyes have seen nor to let them slip from your mind all the days of your life; make them known to your children and your children's children.

—DEUTERONOMY 4:9

Lady Bird Johnson

Lady Bird Johnson is the wife of former president Lyndon B. Johnson. She is an ardent environmentalist, and in 1992, the LBJ Foundation Board of Directors established the Lady Bird Johnson Conservation Award in her honor.

*W*hat better way to celebrate old age than with grandchildren—they bring a richness to life that surpasses all else!

I consider myself the luckiest woman in the world—I had the privilege of watching my seven grandchildren grow into beautiful and productive citizens. And now they are rewarding me with their precious children—my "great grands"—six with two more coming soon!

I wanted to really know my grandchildren, so when they reached an age where they were interesting, I took each on a trip that would appeal to that individual child: white-water rafting, scuba diving in the Virgin Islands, whale watching in Alaska, a trip to Yosemite by train. We had wonderful adventures along with conversations that would not have happened in any other setting. And, oh, what amazing discoveries I made about my darlings! I got to know them as people.

Although age and lack of stamina will not allow me the luxury of travel with my "great grands," they provide more pleasure than I could have imagined! I love watching them play—something I don't believe I did with my grandchildren—and I love their antics and delicious laughter. The "great grands" range in age from two to eight, and I realize this happy innocence is fleeting, and I don't want to miss any of it!

Hazel Jones

Hazel Jones has been a businesswoman and professional photographer and oil colorist for over fifty years. She is coeditor and publisher of The Senior Review *magazine and cohost (along with her daughter, Jan) of* Round the Table with Hazel and Jan, *a radio talk show in Vandalia, Illinois. She was inducted into the Senior Illinois Hall of Fame in 2000.*

GRANDSONS: THE JOYS IN LIFE

*A*h—the joy of the first born grandchild, Zacary, equaled only by the joy of the second born, Gabriel. Each one unique in his own way!

Zac, the four-pound-four-ounce preemie, is now twenty-two years old, stands six feet five inches in his sock feet, has the soul of an artist, and is a budding architectural student. This brown-haired, hazel-eyed charmer never sees anyone as a stranger and spreads his own brand of sunshine wherever he goes. Early in life, he organized the neighborhood kids in their daily play and with his make-believe tools, rebuilt and repaired anything and everything that his imagination decided needed attention. I delighted in his enthusiasm.

Gabe, the blue-eyed blond, has hair that anyone would give their eyeteeth for, and at seventeen is fast approaching the six foot one inch mark. This laid-back young man enjoys music, sings and plays the guitar, and is more than content with his own company. He is extremely talented in both the computer and academic worlds. From the time he was a small boy, dressed in his Superman suit or Teenage Mutant Ninja Turtle garb, doing his own thing, everything has seemed to be effortless. I delighted in his calming nature.

My most cherished gift has been to watch them grow into the fine young men they now are. They are kind, compassionate achievers, who, no matter where they are or whom they are with, are never to busy to call out, "Love you, Mawmaw."

Yes, my grandsons are the special joys in my life . . . and for that I am truly thankful!

❧ ❧

Shirley Jones and Marty Ingels

Shirley Jones is an actress who starred in musical films such as Oklahoma! *and* Carousel. *She was awarded an Academy Award for her role in* Elmer Gantry. *She is also known for her role on the hit television series* The Partridge Family.

Marty Ingels began his career in show business as a stand-up comedian, but later turned his interests toward agency and production. He is the "step"-grandfather to Shirley Jones' grandchildren. The couple has been married since 1977.

GRANDMA VS. GODZILLA
OR
GRANDMA'S IMMORTAL MOMENT

*I*t's not too often we have an opportunity to accurately measure the social rage of a three-year-old. I had one.

1985. I was to work on one of those cruises—Panama Canal, I think. I thought it'd be a nice idea to invite some of my family. Shaun and Ann brought the kids—Caitlin, age three, and Jake, not quite one year.

A few days into the trip, Shaun asked if I'd babysit for a few hours that night while they went to an art auction on board. And there I was, in Shaun's cabin with the two of them. Caitlin was her usual impossible self (a bit more so tonight because I was pacing the room with Jake before putting him down). And it was the old look-at-me-or-else routine that Grandma was never thrilled with. This time she'd dragged out her big old Raggedy Ann doll by its one remaining arm and began swinging it against my leg, which she did the whole time I talked on the phone to her mother.

"No, Cait. You know how Grandma feels about that. Stop that!"

But no. Not Caitlin. The same unyielding independence she would one day take to the Senate floor is in full force tonight, in cabin A41, in the middle of the Atlantic Ocean.

It was clear that somebody in cabin A41 had to show somebody else in cabin A41 who was boss. It was Code Blue—battle stations, furrowed brow, ice-cold stare, and the deepened Vincent Price voice that oozed pictures of the old rack in the great tower.

"Caitlin, I told you to stop."

But Caitlin never missed a Raggedy beat. I grabbed the doll from her grip and began to swat her on the bottom with it.

"How does that feel?" I said over and over. (With no doll-weapon I thought surrender was imminent.) No way. If I was gonna do Vincent Price impressions, she was gonna do Beverly Sills—and I mean peak decibel, rattle-the-chandelier, take-no-breath *screaming*. Hit the secret briefcase button, it was *war*. I grabbed her by the arm and yanked her to the bathroom door.

"Okay, if you're gonna scream, scream in the bathroom all you want. Just let me know when you're finished."

I closed the door and sat just outside waiting for the screaming to subside. And after a time, it did, but Caitlin wasn't coming out, and enough time had lapsed for Field Commander Grandma to blink.

I opened the door, and there she was, sitting on the wide rim of the tub and leaning her face over to the wall, away. I sat on the closed commode and watched her, and wasn't this the perfect Kodak Moment and weren't we the picture: Age & Experience, Authority & Wisdom; History & Knowledge & Truth waiting for a three-year-old weasel with a shattered doll in a metal tub to give me a break. God Bless America.

I leaned toward her and looked to find some bridge between us, some glint of a sign that God's Celestial Plan had a redeeming silver lining after the storm that somehow justified the tears and the turmoil, the angst and the rancor, the shattered dolls and worn-out mamas and stony pouting vigils.

"Do you have anything to say?"

"Do you want to say anything to Grandma?"

"What are you thinking?"

"Talk to me!"

❧ ❧

It seemed an eternity without her moving a muscle. Then, a short, wet sniffle and she slowly gathered herself up from the wall and turned to face me, her little frame holding on to the bathtub rim not ten inches away. It was the sacred moment of truth for both of us. (We had two the day before, and we had one planned for tomorrow.)

I was still talking, trying to get her to come alive. I stopped short of touching her, of pandering to easy physical intermissions for either of us that would only diffuse the serious "lesson" from the encounter we'd just been through, some "learning resolution" we didn't have before. What can I tell you—it was a Grandma lemon-to-lemonade thing.

Suddenly, smack in the middle of one of my sentences, her little lids lifted and tried to manage some focus. Something had caught her eye, and, whatever it was, I was grateful. We were on our way to a post-war epiphany.

I said nothing, and she said nothing. She stayed fixed on something near me, something on me, maybe through me, and I soared inside for my little three-year-old angel who was graduating into Reality and Logic and Life right before my eyes, obviously aware of her date with destiny— Supreme Court Justice Caitlin Cassidy . . . Professor Caitlin Cassidy . . . Ambassador, Lt. Colonel, Surgeon General . . . President Caitlin Cassidy.

And it seemed that . . . wait . . . she's reaching . . . she's lifting her arm and reaching it out toward my shoulder . . . Praise Be, she is actually going to immortalize the moment for always and ever by actually reaching out to her mountain of unconditional love, finally dismissing the whispers of pride and of anger, as if to say I hereby put away my idle toys of . . . wait . . . she's reaching past my shoulder to something on the . . . She is . . . She's stretching to the Commode Flush Button, that's what it is, the Commode Flush Button.

The Commode Flush Button?

Good grief. My surgeon general, my chief justice, my ambassador of strength and stature and delicate humanities, was merely trying to flush me down the toilet, still angry and determined, still clutching her mutilated Raggedy Ann, her one last hope of plain old visceral victory over the Silver Peaked Gulliver, the fierce and final terminator button. It worked for the hairpin and the crayon and the Kleenex; why not for the dastardly Grandma from hell?

That was 1985.

Caitlin Ann Cassidy is today a straight-A student at UCLA, intent, like most of her gang, to find out exactly what makes the world work—or maybe why, in her juncture moment of need a long time ago, the Holland-America plumbing system didn't.

INGELS POINT OF VIEW

In my case (a step) which is sort of a "rep"
  For the Genuine, First-Line, Authentic—
When all's done and said, if the blood guy is Red,
  Then the step guy is kinda "Magentic."

You're "there," but you note, when it comes to a vote
  Comes a certain distinct anonymity;
But, "in on all things," that place "in the wings"
  Has a hidden advantaged proximity—

Which means, in a way, that is to say . . .
  All the family thinks they're "selective":
The grandkids are "Brilliant," and Grandma's
    "Resilient"
  (But only the step guy's "Objective").

For instance, this book takes a tongue-in-cheek look
  At "having the grandchildren first."
It's madness and mirth to poke fun at each birth
  And then having the sequence reversed.

But I saw, in our house, my remarkable spouse
  Have her way with each Cassidy kid;
"What a kick and a blast, if I had those three last"
  . . . What she said—and she actually Did.

Larry Katzman

Larry "Kaz" Katzman is a cartoonist as well as an electrical engineer, inventor, and holder of over one hundred patents and trademarks. His award-winning cartoon, Nellie Nifty, RN, *which combines medicine and laughter, has been featured in newspapers and magazines in over twenty countries. He is also the author of* HeadLines *acrostic-type puzzles.*

I have experienced the first two stages of grandfathering.

Ah, the joys of first-stage grandfathering (from birth to three to four years old):

> I still get my sleep every night!
> I never have to change diapers!
> I never have to feed them!
> I never have to chase after them!
> I never have to take them to nursery school!
> I love them and play with them . . . and then, happily, they go home!

The joys of second-stage grandfathering (from four years old to the teens):

I attend "Grandfather School" while they attend "Grandchild School," especially when they teach me all about computers! (My eight-year-old grandchild expertly flies and lands 747s on a flight simulator program.)

It's a kick to teach them how to ski, to play catch, to play tennis, to cast a fishing line!

It's a kick to turn them into fans of the Mets and the Jets (although I'm not sure whether I'm causing them joy or suffering; one team is at the bottom of the division and the other hasn't been to the Super Bowl since 1969).

It's a kick when one granddaughter loves to draw and wants to be a cartoonist like Grandpa.

"Isn't this ride a bit terrifying for a small boy?"

Bil Keane

Bil Keane is the creator of the award-winning and beloved comic strip The Family Circus. *He is also an author and a former Cartoonist of the Year.*

*W*hile drawing *The Family Circus*, observing our own five children for many years, I wondered where my ideas would come from after they grew up and left home. I needn't have worried.

A whole new bundle of inspiration appeared in our nine grandchildren. They think Granddad is following them around lovingly and I'm out to exploit them!

Being a daddy, with its responsibilities and chores, has made me appreciate how much I have in common with the little grandchildren: afternoon naps, ice cream cones, Disney movies, early bedtimes. What a wonderful world!

"When we have children, Mommy and Daddy
will be promoted to grandparents."

The History of Grandparents Day

· · · · · ·

If you have been dismissing Grandparents Day as just another attempt by department stores to squeeze yet another holiday into their yearly sales, you have missed the point entirely.

In reality, Grandparents Day has its origin in a little West Virginia lady who is so full of love that even the demands of raising fifteen children of her own did not leave her feeling as if she had done enough. That lady is eighty-five-year-old Marian McQuade of Oak Hill.

Marian Herndon McQuade was born in the now-deserted town of Caperton, West Virginia, in 1918. It was an era when neighbors depended on each other, and the elderly and the ill were considered everyone's responsibility. As a child, Marian spent a great deal of time at her grandparents' farm. One of her clearest memories is that every day, after finishing the work on the farm, Marian's grandmother would dress and go out to visit the sick and elderly in the community. These visits were considered not only a responsibility, but also a special joy. For there was magic and wisdom in the memories of these old people that existed nowhere else. This lesson of care and respect for the elderly, which Marian learned from her grandmother, has remained a driving force throughout her life.

When Marian grew to womanhood, she married her longtime sweetheart, Joe McQuade. Together they raised fifteen strong, healthy children. But Marian never forgot her grandmother's example, which had shown her that responsibility for others does not end on your own doorstep. As her children grew to adulthood, Marian continued to do what she could to ease the loneliness of the elderly who touched her life.

She did this in a variety of ways. Beginning in 1956, she was an active worker on the Past Eighty Party, which was originated by Jim Comstock, editor of the *West Virginia Hillbilly*. In 1971, she was elected vice chairman of the West Virginia Commission on Aging.

Anywhere that a group was working for the rights and benefits of the elderly, Marian McQuade was ready and willing to serve. Over the years she has held positions as the president of the Vocational Rehabilitation Foundation, vice president of the West Virginia Health Systems Agency, a member of the Nursing Home Licensing Board and cochairman of the Bi-Centennial Centenarian Search for the West Virginia Commission on Aging.

In her spare time, she regularly visited with the elderly in area nursing homes and was well aware of the joy that such visits brought to them. It was on one of these visits that something happened which intensified her already strong sense of responsibility for the elderly.

During her visits to a particular nursing home, she noticed one woman who always seemed to remain apart from the others. It was obvious that this quiet little lady spent the majority of her time alone. Marian made a special effort to include this shy woman in whatever activity was arranged for the day. As Marian prepared to leave at the end of one visit, the lady grasped her hand and whispered, "Please come back again."

Surprised and touched by the plea, Marian assured her that she would definitely come back often to see her. It broke her heart when the lady dropped her hand and sadly whispered, "No, you won't. Everybody says that, but they never do."

That day, Marian McQuade swore to herself that she would do her best not only to brighten the life of this one lonely lady, but to help bring joy to all those who fear they are forgotten.

However, no matter how active she was, Marian was haunted by the feeling that there was only so much she personally could do. So she decided to take her campaign to ease the loneliness of the elderly to the public.

Never one to beat around the bush, her first step was a direct call to West Virginia Governor Arch Moore in February of 1973. She outlined to him her idea of designating a special day in honor of the elderly people who have given so much during their lifetimes and often get so little in return. She explained to him that she felt a day should be set aside when people across the state would be encouraged to remember and visit the elderly.

Moore was immediately supportive of the idea but before the event could be made official, it needed a name. Marian decided to call it Grandparents Day because, as she says, "Everyone may not be a grandparent, but everyone is a grandchild. So this would be a day in which everyone could become involved."

Governor Moore agreed and he issued a special proclamation establishing the first Grandparents Day in May of 1973, but Marian was not content to limit her campaign to the boundaries of West Virginia. She immediately began writing to governors of other states urging similar proclamations. Then she found a better way to take it a step further.

She had gained the support of Senator Jennings Randolph for her project. Together, he and Marian decided that September would be the best time of year in which to honor those in the "autumn" of life. In 1973, Senator Randolph introduced a resolution to the United States Senate. Five years later, in 1978, Congress unanimously passed legislation proclaiming the first Sunday after Labor Day as National Grandparents Day.

That day Marian McQuade received an official telephone call from the White House informing her that her bill had been signed by President Carter and Grandparents Day was now a national holiday.

Marian's work was far from finished. For over twenty years after the legislation passed, she continued to work tirelessly to promote greater attention for the elderly. As official founder of Grandparents Day, she was constantly in demand as a speaker to explain the significance of the event. Her website, *www.grandparentsday.com*, receives over 300,000 hits each month from all over the United States from those who want information on the holiday.

Each response stresses that Grandparents Day is meant to be more than just a formality. It is important that people take the opportunity to share the strength, guidance, and love that the elderly have to give. Marian hopes that those who no longer have grandparents of their own will participate by visiting local nursing homes and easing the loneliness which so often prevails there.

The echo of that one lonely woman's plea still lives on in her heart. That one event planted a seed that continues to grow today. Marian kept her promise to that lonely little lady in the nursing home in a way that no one could ever have foreseen.

She not only continued to visit the elderly and lonely; she brought the nation with her.

—Written by Shirley Love

  Shirley Love has been a West Virginia state senator since 1994. He is also a member of the National Grandparents Day Council's Founder's Advisory Committee.

. . . . . .

> No cowboy was ever faster on the draw than a
> grandparent pulling a baby picture out of a wallet.
>
> —ANONYMOUS

Harmon Killebrew

*Harmon Killebrew played baseball for the Minnesota Twins
during a career that spanned three decades. Known for his
awesome hitting power, he was named an American League
All-Star thirteen times and was inducted into the National
Baseball Hall of Fame in 1984.*

"MOMMY, AN OLD BALD MAN TRIED TO DROWN ME!"
OR
ATTACK OF THE TWO-FOOT TUB NESS MONSTER!

*E*leven and a half years ago, my relatively new wife,
Nita, and I decided to take on the daunting task of
babysitting my eighteen-month-old grandson, Garrett, for
two weeks while his parents vacationed out of the country.
Garrett was tall and incredibly thin as he chose soon after
birth to follow a vegetarian diet and went through great gy-

rations to explain exactly what he would like to eat at each meal. By the time we guessed the right item, we were all too exhausted to eat! Anyway, I decided Garrett needed a bath. He evidently thought otherwise. He profoundly said, "No, Papa." I said, "Yes, Garrett. You've been swimming in the pool all day and we need to rinse you off." He again firmly stated, "No, Papa!" My wife said, "Just let him be for a little while and we'll bathe him before bedtime." I, just as firmly as my midget grandson, said, "NO, he needs a bath NOW!" My infinitely wise (and growing more wise every minute) wife said, "Well, big guy, you're on your own. I'm going to vacuum the living room."

I thought, well he's only eighteen months old, two feet tall, and must weigh no more than twenty pounds. I on the other hand was an almost six foot (rapidly aging) former home-run hitter. I figured I had at least 180 pounds on this little rookie. I promptly filled our giant jetted master bathtub with water and proceeded to un-diaper this scrawny little dwarf. He immediately started screaming at the top of his lungs and throwing himself into all sorts of distorted pretzel-like shapes. Taking my challenge for clean grandchildren very seriously, I proceeded to toss him in the tub and thoroughly douse him as well as myself from head to foot with water. His screaming escalated to a high-pitched shrill that sounded vaguely like police sirens. I managed to get him soaped up and his hair thoroughly sudsed and was trying diligently to get him rinsed. Dang, that little guy was truly *impossible* to handle when he was slippery. I, the once great Harmon Killebrew, was going to have to admit defeat.

However, as I tried to get the little bugger to hold still so the soap wouldn't get in his eyes, I felt myself getting weaker and suddenly short of breath. I tried to call out to my far, far away wife who was vacuuming, "Nita, help me. Nita help!" My voice was incredibly weak. By some stroke of luck, Nita heard what she thought was an odd bird chirping and turned off the vacuum. Again, I tried to get her attention as I clung desperately to this writhing and screaming alien namesake of mine. Nita finally opened the bathroom door and said, "Are you okay in here?" I was pale and felt myself rapidly running out of air. I said, "Nita, I think I'm having a heart attack. Help me." She actually started laughing. Not just a little laugh, but a hysterical laugh. I'd never heard her laugh like that, so I *knew* I was having a heart attack. She came over and in one swoop, grabbed the Tub Ness Monster squirming frantically in my hands and dipped him once or twice (my vision was blurring) under the faucet and snatched him out of the tub and proceeded to dry him off. I sat on the floor exhausted and spent, leaning against the tub. Suddenly my vision returned and my breathing followed. What! Was this just an anxiety attack? Could this possibly be? I was nailed to the bathmat by a slippery, slimy infant. So much for Hall of Fame statistics!

"I'LL POO-POO AT MY MOMMA'S HOUSE"

Actually, only twelve months after that bathtub incident, my ever brave and valiant wife and I decided to give it another try watching Garrett, now two and a half years old, for another ten days while his geniusparents vacationed this time in the Fiji Islands. After getting furtive instructions on how we frequently needed to ask Garrett if he needed to go poo-poo, I figured I had this down pat. After all, I survived the attack of the two-foot Tub Ness Monster.

Per our instructions, I followed little Garrett around diligently asking him if he needed to go poo-poo—for four days! He always said, "No, Papa!" Well, I'm not a slow learner. I took the little man at his word. But four days! Wow! According to our written instructions, this little man should have been chucking out "poo-poos" at the rate of two to three times a day! I was worried. So at the end of day four I really followed him *everywhere!* "Garrett, do you need to go poo-poo?" "Garrett, do you need to go poo-poo in the potty?" "Garrett, come on, let's go poo-poo." "Garrett, let's play a fun, sit on the potty poker game." "Garrett, you *need to go poo-poo.*" That was the last straw. This still-scrawny runt turned around with a very defiant stance, placed his hands on his waist and stated very loudly and firmly so as to penetrate my thick ever-aging and balding skull, *"Leave me alone, Papa! I'll go poo-poo at my Momma's house."*

I was dumbfounded. I had been told. He intended to

wait ten days to complete his manly duties. I had a truly newfound respect for this little guy. I mean, I for one didn't like public restrooms, but even I had never held it for ten days! I left him alone, and he promptly went into my ever-loving wife's sewing room, crouched down behind her rocking chair and pooped!

Garrett 2, Papa 0.

Evel Knievel

Evel Knievel is the most famous motorcycle daredevil of all time. Known for his outrageous tricks and stunts, he can boast clearing a jump over thirteen semitrucks and attempting to jump such wide valleys as the Snake River Canyon.

I have nine grandchildren and one great-grandchild. I have my two oldest granddaughters, Robbie's daughters, Carmen and Kristen. They're in their early twenties and both pursuing education. (My great granddaughter's named Analise. She's Carmen's daughter.) Kelly has a daughter named Shelley, so that's three. Alicia has a daughter named Jaicee, that's my fourth. But my oldest daughter, Tracy, has the other five of the nine—Josiah, Jesse, Melody,

Cody, and Cole. That's four boys and one sweet, little girl.

While on vacation this summer in Montana, I went to visit them. They all race bicycle motocross at track in Bozeman, Montana. And, every summer, a lot of the motocross racers from all across the state of Montana come to race there. Sometimes over 200 come. I mean 200—that's a lot! Every single one of the five grandchildren (and they are aged fourteen to three), won the main event for the state qualifier in their age class, even my little granddaughter Melody.

The littlest one, Cole, he rode around the track, too. It's a pretty lengthy track over bumps and jumps and corners. He is so little that they couldn't find a helmet to fit him. The only one they could find to fit him was a full coverage helmet. It was so big he had to look out underneath the bottom of the helmet.

And they're all so good. Cody, the second youngest, said to me, "I don't like to race against Melody. She beats all the boys."

Josiah and Jesse play golf during the summertime. They all are big skiers in the wintertime. They also race motorcycles on the racetrack and they fish and hunt and skateboard, but the main thing they seem to have a lot of expertise in is the trampoline. They have one in their backyard. Their dad, Mitch, oversees everything they do—he's a great dad.

I enjoy going on vacation in Montana for one or two

months every summer. I enjoy being with them during the summer, watching them grow. It's quite an experience.

I'll admit that sometimes they do things I wish they wouldn't because I'm afraid of them getting hurt, either on the track or in daily life—even just crossing a street. I can just imagine the things mothers and dads used to worry about when their kids saw me on television. Even now, I have kids come up to me once or twice a week and say, "My mom and dad used to get mad when I said I was trying to be Evel Knievel." Now, as a grandparent, I'm finally experiencing what other mothers and fathers have felt and I apologize for putting them through all the hell I did.

I'm so very proud of each of my grandkids. I wish every grandparent could have grandchildren like I have and experience and enjoy the pride I have in their wonderful lust for life. They all seem to have it.

⌦∘⌦∘⌦

Janet Krauss

Janet Krauss is a poet whose work has appeared in Plainsongs, American Goat, Spoon River Quarterly, Jewish Currents, *and* College English. *She is an adjunct professor at Fairfield University.*

FAITH IN THE NEWBORN

The only other time my husband called me at work was a year ago to tell me momentous news. The news was my mother-in-law's death, which we were expecting. This year's news was the birth of our first grandchild. Of course, I was elated over the latter, but felt thrown back in time: the cold strangeness of the tragedy mingled with my present ecstasy. And hearing my husband's voice filled with emotion blended with my memory of his voice last year. The sequence of events dramatically demonstrated the cycles of birth and death.

I recall the poet Wallace Stevens' words when he smoothly linked the opposites' coexistence together: "Death is the mother of beauty, mystical, / Within whose burning bosom we devise / Our earthly mothers waiting, sleeplessly." Contraries must exist to appreciate one from another, to appreciate and understand the balance between them, especially between life and death.

After the initial impact of the news, I let joy take over. The reactions of my friends at work moved me. Rachel's birth belonged to all: The women recalled their labor pains or nurtured hopes of becoming grandmothers; the men recalled their anxieties. All these recollections and personal wishes were expressed with pure joyousness. It felt as if my friends washed themselves with the hope that Rachel brought into the world. She became our talisman.

In her letter, my friend Lynda movingly declared that

universal faith in the newborn: "Think of the lifeline—the threads your family is weaving. . . . I've always thought that with a newborn the spirit of generations awakens. A new baby being born into the world is like something letting loose and forming a connectedness at the same time."

The nativity-like scene in my daughter-in-law's hospital room twelve hours after she gave birth confirmed my friend's words. The two sets of grandparents stood on each side of the bed, faces mirroring each other's unequivocal bliss as the young mother held her baby, a triumphant smile on her tired face. My son was at her side. When he held his daughter, I felt the force of generations, the ongoing-ness of the life urge, the repetition of family scenarios.

As I adjust to my new role and place in the scheme of the family, I study the phenomenon of my granddaughter's arrival. As she still retains infancy, Rachel's luminous face displays an otherworldliness, a knowledge she seems to have come with that I will never know, perhaps a peace unknown to me.

That otherworldliness can be compared to the mystical one the Magi experienced before the Christ child. As T. S. Eliot wrote in his poem "The Journey of the Magi," the Magi had encountered a birth and a death when they found Jesus. They experienced a birth of hope in a new religious sense and a death of old ways of believing. For me, Rachel's birth made it easier to accept the flow of life and death: The blessing of this year alleviated the family tragedy of last year.

When I took my oldest friends to see Rachel, all four desired to hold her. We stood in a circle passing the baby from one's arms to another's—our talisman, and a fresh, new source of connectedness.

—FIRST PUBLISHED BY JANET KRAUSS IN *WESTPORT NEWS*, JANUARY 14, 1987.

In order to influence a child, one must be careful not to be that child's parent or grandparent.

—DON MARQUIS

Think not forever of yourselves, O Chiefs, nor of your own generation. Think of continuing generations of our families, think of our grandchildren and of those yet unborn, whose faces are coming from beneath the ground.

—PEACEMAKER, CREATOR OF THE IROQUOIS CONFEDERACY, AROUND 1000 AD.

Julius LaRosa

Julius LaRosa is a singer and entertainer. His career began in 1951 after he left the Navy. It soon blossomed to include performances at New York's famous Carnegie Hall.

The day after my daughter was born I had an appointment with an associate who was my senior by many years. Rushing into his office, I shouted, "Dave! Dave! Rory had the baby! A girl! She was six pounds and—" He cut me off. "Shut up!" he said. "You don't know nothin' till you have your first grandchild!" Now I know . . .

My grandson, Robert Terence Smith, Jr. (we call him Lil' Ter), is an enchanting, brilliant, and remarkably sensitive soon-to-be-six-year-old child. He calls me "Papa Joolie" and I faint! I was born on the second day of January 1930, and for as long as I can remember I've said I wanted to live to be seventy so I could say I lived in two centuries. I made it, but have now asked for an extension to 2020 so I can be at my grandson's college graduation!

A favorite story: Last year I was away for two months, and several days later Lil' Ter asked his mother, my daughter Maria, "When is Papa Joolie coming home?" She answered, "He won't be home 'til April, sweetheart." In the days and weeks that followed, Lil' Ter would ask regularly, "Is it April yet, Mommy?"

On the other hand, my grandmother loved to say, "Grandparents have all the joys and none of the woes." Huh? She'd then go through a litany of "You do's" to the parents of her grandchildren: "You do the feeding, you do the diapers, you do the getting up in the middle of the night, you do the disciplining; just let me do love and bring presents. When you come to visit me, don't come without the baby! Then, when you leave, don't leave *without* the baby!"

Patrick Leahy

Patrick J. Leahy was elected to the United States Senate in 1974. A Democrat from Vermont, he is a senior member of the Appropriations Committee and has worked to ban landmines and protect privacy and civil liberties. He is perhaps best known around Capitol Hill as the "cyber senator" for his intimacy with Internet legislation.

$\mathcal{M}$arcelle and I are blessed to have two grandchildren—one five years old and the other nine months.

When I think about children today, I am amazed by their computer literacy. When our grandson was four years old, he came into my den and asked if I could access a certain children's website. This site allowed interactive involvement where the user could add pictures, do treasure hunts, and so forth. I typed in the appropriate website address and it came up. At that point, my grandson, Roan, climbed into my lap, took the mouse out of my hand, and said, "I should take over now, Grandpa. This gets very complicated!"

I may be a U.S. senator, but this four-year-old knew exactly what the standards were.

Leon Lederman

Leon M. Lederman was a co-recipient of the Nobel Prize in Physics in 1988. He taught at the University of Chicago and worked for the state of Illinois developing programs to train teachers to teach math and science.

*O*nce upon a time, children grew up with grandparents in the house or on the next street. Today, there is an instantaneous diaspora as young adults move out for college or distant employment and rarely come back. The visit to grandma and grandpa is a ritual I remember from my own young parent days when daughter Rachel, commenting on heavy Sunday traffic, would comment, "Look at all the people who are going to Grandma's house!"

So I made the mistake of blinking my eyes and, flash!, I have four grandkids—two younger ones, Raziel (three years old) and Izak (six years old), on the West Coast and two on the East Coast, Jayna (twelve years old) and Evan (seventeen years old). And I live on the midwestern coast of Lake Michigan.

Ellen and I get two visits a year from each pair: winter skiing from our vacation house in Driggs, Idaho, and summer hiking, talking, swimming also in and around the Tetons. The West Coast pair are too young to know in our brief assemblies, but teenagers are much easier.

Jayna is the humorist and she tries valiantly to match Grandpa in story- and joke-telling. And she is quick. I said, "A termite walks into a bar and asks, 'Where is the bartender?'"

She says, "Oh, I get it! A man runs into a bar. 'Ouch!'"

Jayna will conquer if she can keep her sense of humor.

Evan is a philosopher. His input-output machinery is hampered, but the central processor works fine.

Evan is dyslexic and has had extraordinary help, both from the Princeton Public Schools and from Mom, a Princeton professor. Evan is, thanks to these aids, a high school senior, and is coming out with a multitude of interests: drama, film, history, politics, and the saving grace of a knack for putting his beliefs in a humorous vein. Just a very concise example of a grandson's style, he writes in a college application form a quasi-fictional exchange with a colleague: "Pulling out my notebook I said, 'I could use some help with my spelling. I want to explain in this part that I am dyslexic, but I can't spell that word.'

" 'D-Y-S-L-E-X-I-C.'

" 'Thanks, that problem does slow me up a bit, but I refuse to let it limit my imagination. Apart from that, the story is coming along nicely.' "

From this sample, all must agree that this is a guy one would have loved to have known much, much earlier and (choke, sigh) way, way later.

Brenda Lee

Brenda Lee is an accomplished musician. She is the first woman to have been inducted into both the Country Music Hall of Fame (in 1997) and the Rock and Roll Hall of Fame (in 2002). Her record sales exceed 100 million.

"MEEMAW" KNOWS BEST

*I*t's been said many times, "There is absolutely no substitute for experience," but never did this truth become more meaningful to me than when I became a grandmother. I, like most, had been "tested by fire" and thereby successfully learned many of life's important parenting lessons. Without a doubt, I knew the proper path, the most effective child-rearing rules.

So, offered here are just a few pearls of wisdom that may help some frazzled parents . . . a sneak peek into "Meemaw's" house.

* Discipline is non-existent and quite unnecessary in a home of uninterrupted hugs and laughter. Should my grandchildren act unbecoming on occasion, most any thoughtful person would certainly realize that, "They are just overly tired."

* Messes are overlooked. Carpets can be cleaned, spilled milk wiped up, and scattered toys gathered in a minute. And that broken, 100-year-old Imari vase? Well, it was just an old vase, after all.

* Missing school is an option every now and again, especially on warm, sunny mornings when a child's thoughts of being cooped up in school are akin to death. I can almost promise that the college admissions director will never know the difference.

* Watching videos together for hours on end is encouraged. For example, knowing every single line

and song to Disney's *Aladdin* and happily chanting them together on cue somehow seems good for the soul.

* Clothes are always my grandchildren's choice, much to the chagrin of their parents. Would we prefer the fancy smocked dresses from London? Oh no! Not us. We prefer the comfortable, the tacky, the colorful, the mismatched.

* Baths are kept at a minimum and only taken when absolutely necessary. A good swipe of the face, hands, and feet before bed, and we're good as new.

* Dinner time is always a festive, talkative, lingering affair, and food rules never apply. If you try it and don't like it, so be it. We have plenty of pre-packaged, processed, fun foods always on hand.

The list goes on and on, the important and seemingly unimportant. It's a mental list I've adopted by *unlearning and undoing* everything I was, everything I did, as a parent. And, yes, I am wiser, but not necessarily because of the number of years that have passed. Just realizing what truly matters most is the simple, yet often missed, secret. And seeing life through the eyes of a child combined with self-assurance, patience and lots of love are key ingredients.

So, are you ready to get cookin'? Good. I'll race ya!!

Len Lesser

Len Lesser is an actor who is perhaps best remembered for his role as Jerry's Uncle Leo on the Emmy Award—winning comedy Seinfeld. *He has appeared on film and television for over forty years and now stars in* Everybody Loves Raymond.

I came to grandfatherhood rather late, being seventy-six when my first grandchild was born. So I really haven't had that much time to be with four-year-old Jonathan and Kayla, who is two and a half.

What has impressed me most are the changes that occur in a child after birth. It's quite exciting and really very enlightening to watch the monthly changes in little people (learning to talk, walk, relate to others, developing their personalities, etc.). Since grandparenthood is "all play and no work," I usually have a lovely time being with them.

Of course, they have their moods and needs and at times can be difficult and willful—they of course are testing their limits. But most of the time, I find myself smiling for hours and enjoying their company immensely.

Children can be open and delightful and beautiful and they keep me young. Joy to the world!

Art Linkletter

Art Linkletter is an Emmy and Grammy Award—winning entertainer and a best-selling author. He hosted the television program Kids Say the Darndest Things, *based on his best-selling book. His many honors include being named Grandfather of the Year in 1962.*

God gave us grandchildren as a reward for growing old. He also knew how happy we could be to see our children learn the hard way what we suffered through with them. Lois and I now have eight grandchildren and fifteen great-grandchildren.

Each generation has been a great education for us in different ways, i.e., the first child-with-bloody-nose was rushed to the nearest emergency hospital. The fifth child-with-bloody-nose was told to get out in the yard immediately and stop bleeding on the carpet. When our first son was "bad" (at seventeen), we took away the keys to his car for a week as punishment. When the first grandson (at seventeen) was guilty of breaking some family rules, my son put him to bed without his girl. Times change!

In my lifetime, we experienced tremendous change, in every way imaginable. But parenting is still a mystery. Every child is unique. Every stage in a child's life differs in special ways. Basically, the first ten years is a time when the children are asking "Why?" and "What?" In the next ten years, the parents are asking, "What is happening to our baby?"

Friends become more important in the middle teens than almost anything else. You can't choose his friends and you probably won't choose his future wife, much less his girlfriends.

Grandchildren, on the other hand, welcome the loving admiration of their grandparents and often flee to them to escape the parental efforts to control their lives.

So grandparents must learn to walk a shaky diplomatic road as referees and even coaches to guide the new parents along the teen roller-coaster age.

Great-grandchildren are even easier. Just spoil them in every way you can and pray for the best!

Frank Mancuso

Frank G. Mancuso is the director and former CEO of Metro-Goldwyn-Mayer Studios.

*W*hen I was asked if I wanted to participate in this book I didn't have to think about it much past reading what the title was going to be. I thought, "How absolutely perfect." It's more than a book title; it is a life experience. My wife and I have two children who have seven offspring. They and their spouses are responsible for the unique joy in our lives—our grandchildren.

On several occasions, I have heard friends or associates say, "I'd like to start life over, but know what I know today." Indeed, that's exactly what we have the opportunity to do through our grandchildren. By sharing with them, small doses at a time of course, the lessons and experiences we have learned and earned in life, we are starting over through them.

I know, in our case, my wife and I were married and became parents too young to have accumulated much of life's wisdom. So it was "on the job" training being a couple and parents. Judging by the quality human beings our daughter and son have become, we didn't do too badly after all.

But oh, the joy and fun of grandchildren! Our seven precious jewels range in age from two to fifteen years old and the art of acting and playing at their age level is a constant source of happiness. It is a welcome change from the formal business environment I worked in for so many years. And that is exactly the point—it is not just what we can give to our grandchildren, but how much our grandchildren can give back to us. As we share our knowledge with them, they give to us their innocence, youth, energy, and uncomplicated love. It's difficult to describe how different the experience is with each of them, with their diverse personalities, sensitivities, sense of humor, and emotionality. The challenge and, at the same time, pleasure of nurturing each of these growing, developing human beings that are a part of your family tree is indeed the essence of life. It is easier to devote the time to them as grandparents when you have less of the demands on your life. It's also great that at the end of the visit they go home so you can recharge your battery.

We have what we call the "command attendance Sunday" when the entire Mancuso clan comes to our home for Sunday dinner and conversation. It also allows us to celebrate special occasions like birthdays and anniversaries together at one of the Sunday dinners. With all the practice, I have noticed how much better the grandchildren have gotten at blowing out candles and singing "Happy Birthday." But, ultimately it is about the conversation with all of them, not only with us, but that which they have with each other that is the most memorable part of our Sunday family dinners. We are never more than seven days behind what goes on in their lives at school, in sports, or who the new best friend is, and it is quite amazing to see how attached the seven cousins have become. These are the things that family traditions are made of.

I hope that establishing and maintaining that kind of

communication will make them feel that they can come to us to discuss at anytime anything that is going on in their lives. We also hope that many years from now, when they have their own children, they will tell them the stories about how every Sunday they would go with their parents to "Amma and Papa's house" and what wonderful times they had and how it was the best day of the week. Well, I hope it happens that way, but if it doesn't, it will still be the best day of the week for Amma and Papa.

Willard on What's So Good About Being a Grandchild?

. . . . . .

Grandparents spoil you rotten.

You can learn about history firsthand.

You can learn funny family tales about your parents as kids.

The rules are a lot more flexible at Grandma and Grandpa's house.

Grandpa likes ice cream, too.

DJ McQuade

DJ McQuade is the daughter of Marian McQuade, the founder of National Grandparents Day. She is also the coordinator of the National Grandparents Day Council.

FROM THE JOURNAL OF DJ MCQUADE

*A*ugust 7, 2003—My ten-year-old granddaughter came to visit from Seattle today. Her Aunt Robin and I met her plane. When she walked through the gate, I got goose bumps. Carly looks exactly like a picture of my mother at that age.

And what a charmer! Not only does she look like my mother; she has her bright-wire personality. Of course, my daughter Jenni warned us before the visit that Carly can exhibit a rather "hard head." Now where could she have gotten that?

Carly's mother, I seem to remember, wrote me when she was in Marine Corps training, that she was being "exposed to various forms of corrective discipline" for what they termed her "willfulness." And when my own mother was growing up, that same headstrong trait in her was identified as "stubbornness." Definitely in the family genes.

When we pulled into the driveway, Carly waited while I took several new Grandparents of the Year nominations from the mailbox. Later, I wanted to show each one to her and tell her all about why each had been nominated. But Carly was only mildly interested. Being the great-granddaughter of the Founder of National Grandparents Day doesn't really register on her radar screen. As with any ten-year-old, she's more interested in Auntie Robin's Game Boy.

August 8, 2003—We went to the water park today—just Carly and me and my scooter.

We went straight to the wave pool, and Carly swam for the deep end with easy strokes. I rode nervously from one end of the pool to the other, certain that the other bathers' inner tubes would catch Carly in between them and she'd be held underwater.

But she danced. And she dove. And she stood on her hands and kicked her feet and caught the waves, oblivious to everyone and everything except the cool water. Reminds me of how much her mother loves the water. A water baby at nine months old, she would scream in protest when I took her out of the pool. When she was a water ballet student at age fifteen, I was working and didn't get to watch her at practice. Ah, another advantage to being a grandmother—you have the time to be there.

August 9, 2003—Carly wanted to play on the computer until it was time to go to the zoo. I told her that the computer was our Grandparents-website-workhorse and that I needed to scan in the new Grandparents of the Year entries. But I could show her the webpage with a picture of her mother at age four, plus her Aunt Robin at age two, with their grandfather. Now she was showing some interest.

I asked if she knew when the first Grandparents Day was celebrated. Nope. "Thirty years ago," I said. "In West Virginia. Because your great-grandmother, Marian McQuade, started it all. First we had a Mother's Day for kids to show appreciation to their mothers, then we had a Father's Day. But Marian McQuade wanted a day to honor grandparents. She had visited lots of nursing homes where old people were sick and lonesome and sad. And nobody came to visit them. And my mother wanted people to love their grandparents enough to visit them all the time."

Carly was now listening intently. I showed her a picture of Maude Dickerson, my mother's grandmother. I told her that it was actually Marian's grandmother who taught her to value old people. And I tried to paint the picture of Marian as a girl, spending her summers on her grandmother's farm. In the afternoons, Marian would run alongside Granny Dickerson as she traipsed through the woods and across the creeks to visit elderly people at their farmhouses. I explained that some of the old people were sick and Marian and her grandmother took them food and home remedies. That's what neighbors did for each other back then.

I couldn't tell by Carly's expression how much was registering.

August 10, 2003—Robin and her husband, Paul, picked us up for the Tour d' Elegance at Eastlake. Robin and I were enthralled at the prospect of seeing homes and furnishings that only millionaires could afford.

Before we got out of the car, Robin said, "Okay, Carly, the rule is that you stay where I can see you. You don't have to stay with me, but I don't want to have to be looking for you all the time and I don't want anything to happen to you."

Several times, we looked around and no Carly. Usually when we found her, she had gravitated to a swimming pool or fountain and was sampling the water. We would remind her again that she was to stay within sight and also not to put any part of her body in the swimming pools or fountains. Minutes later, I saw Carly playing in yet another fountain. Later, when Carly asked for ice cream, Aunt Robin said, "No, because you didn't stay within sight. I had to go looking for you too many times."

After supper, Carly and I took the dogs to the park. As we played, she seemed downcast. I asked her what she thought of not getting ice cream. She said, "Well, I don't think Aunt Robin likes me as much now because I have a hard head."

"You came by it honestly," I told her. "All the way from your great-great-grandmother and your great-grandmother and your mother. Actually, I might have—*might* have been—stubborn myself when I was ten. And when I was eleven. And twelve. And I got in trouble for it, too. And probably I'm still hardheaded and stubborn . . ."

Jeez, I'm thinking. This grandparenting is not so easy. How can I get Carly to understand that having a hard head doesn't mean you're a bad person or unlikable? Or a loser?

I sent her to chase after the dogs until I could think of a way to explain things. When she got back, I had it. Good ol' Dale Carnegie: "When you have a lemon, make a lemonade." So I told Carly to pretend that willfulness and hardheadedness and stubbornness are like the juice from a lemon. If you serve up the juice with no sweetener, it's pretty sour. Add just a little sweetener, and the willfulness and hardheadedness and stubbornness become determination and perseverance and persistence—tasty lemonade!

"We probably wouldn't even have a Grandparents Day if your great-grandmother wasn't so stubborn. She simply wouldn't give up. Do you think they just said, 'Oh, you want a special holiday for grandparents? Here it is.' Nope. For over eight years, Marian wrote letters to four governors and senators and made speeches and served on boards and had to convince many, many people to be on her side. But she was hardheaded and persistent and determined. And she did it!"

I asked Carly, "So what are you going to do with your lemony hard head?"

She answered, "I'm going to get a holiday for kids and that will be a special day when all kids can break as many rules as they want!"

What could I say?

August 11, 2003—At the ceramics store, Robin, Carly, and I chose our pieces to paint. Carly chose a little frog with a big smile. We were engrossed in our projects when we noticed Carly not painting. "Are you finished?" A storm was brewing on her face. She abruptly stood up and left the table. We called her back. It turned out that the black paint had smeared on the frog's mouth. "Oh, don't worry," Auntie Robin said. "You can just wash that off and redo the mouth. He's too cute to give up on. Why don't you try again?"

Carly picked up the frog and looked at me uncertainly. I said, "Do you think this could be one of those lemonade moments?" She took the frog to the sink, washed its mouth, and repainted it. She smiled with satisfaction. "I didn't give up," she said. "I persisted." I don't know which of us was happier.

Robin didn't get the lemonade part but she knew that a light had gone on in a certain little girl's head. This definitely deserved a celebration; so we trekked across the mall to the ice cream parlor and chowed down on hot fudge sundaes.

August 13, 2003—We took Carly to Farrell's last night, the final evening of her visit. She was telling knock-knock jokes and enjoying all the attention. Today, at 2 P.M., she boarded the plane back to Seattle. We told her mother that next summer, we want her here longer. Why? Because it was fun.

And I have just one more thing to say:

Thank you, Mother, for giving grandparents their due—and their day. And thank you, grandchildren, for making every day Grandparents Day.

Ray Meyer

Ray Meyer, a Basketball Hall of Famer, played for the University of Notre Dame. He was also the head coach at DePaul University.

I really can't say if I would have been a grandparent first. We had six children; three boys and three girls. Our first child was something special. Then they came along one by one. They grew up and married.

Then came the grandchildren. God bless them all. Susan was the first. I had forgotten the joy and happiness I had with my own children. It hit me like a bombshell. Susan was part of me and my family. I am a grandfather! I began to spend a lot of time at my daughter's house. I loved to hold the baby and every time she cried I picked her up. I cradled her, rocked her, and walked with her. My daughter was upset because I showered her with affection and I was spoiling her very badly. Susan wanted to be held and my daughter had trouble putting her down to sleep. I wasn't allowed to pick her up when she cried. This was the first grandchild and then they started coming one after another and now I have seventeen grandchildren! I loved to hold all of them and play with them on my lap when they were very young. As they grew older, I played outdoors with them.

They were growing older and so was I. It was getting difficult for Grandpa to chase them around and play with them. And I found it difficult to get to all their games, recitals, and parties.

I attended all their graduations—grade school, high school, and college. It seemed there was at least one graduation every June.

The happiest day of the year was Christmas Day. I always had Christmas at my house and the whole family would be there. We exchanged gifts. I played Santa Claus for a while. I had the grandchildren sit on my lap next to the tree and I would give them their presents. I gave up being Santa Claus when my older grandchildren would say, "Thanks Grandpa" instead of "Thanks Santa."

I solved the shopping problems after my wife died. I

told all the mothers to buy the gifts for their children and I wrote them checks on Christmas Day. This way, the children received what they wanted. I always remember the joy the grandchildren had when they opened their gifts. Their mothers would spend precious time wrapping their gifts and they ripped the paper savagely to get them. Then when they received their gifts they would go from one gift to another. They couldn't make up their minds which one they wanted to play with.

Grandchildren, I love them all! The grandchildren married, and now I have ten great-grandchildren and I'm starting over.

Our children are not going to be just our children. They are going to be other people's husbands and wives and the parents of our grandchildren.

—MARY CALDERONE

Marjorie Margolies-Mezvinsky

The Honorable Marjorie Margolies-Mezvinsky was the first woman elected to Congress from the state of Pennsylvania. She now lectures at the University of Pennsylvania on government with an interest in women's studies.

*W*hen I was asked to contribute to this book, I thought, What fun, I love to tell grandchildren stories. Then I thought about the many, many times I sat listening to my friends regale, rejoice, hyperbolize—tell grandchildren stories. I laughed, I smiled. "Okay," I thought, "Why would they think this is interesting?"

And I promised myself I wouldn't be one of those grandparents who carried pictures—instead I do a slide show.

I've become a part of the lunatic grandparent fringe, and as boomers start to become grandparents, the fringe will become a *tidal wave*. We have one of those "his, hers, ours, theirs" families. I adopted two girls before I married, married into four girls, had two boys, then became the legal guardian to three more. From this fertile gaggle, there are twelve grandchildren.

One of my grandchildren, Lucas Maiman (then five years old), loves coins. I was able to set up a tour of the U.S. Mint in Philadelphia. With us was Luke's mother and his (then three-year-old) sister Ryan. As we got into the lobby, Ryan, who was unusually excited about this visit, said, "So where are the mints? I love mints."

In most cases, I believe, one smiles, one is polite—but one is thinking, "You have to have been there." But one of my grandmother-friends did have two darling, politically correct stories that I'll relate.

Her daughter took her three-year-old into the voting booth—the judge said, "Isn't it cute! She's voting." The three-year-old said, "My mother says if you don't vote, you can't complain."

Another one of her children was lighting candles outside after 9/11. Her two-and-a-half-year-old asked why she was doing it. Her mom said, "To show God's love." And the little girl said, "Do you think She can see all of us?"

Sue Myrick

Sue Myrick has long been prominent in both business and politics. Before taking office in the House of Representatives as a representative from North Carolina in 1994, she was president and CEO of Myrick Advertising and Public Relations and was the first woman mayor of Charlotte, North Carolina.

When our grandson, Jake, was two years old we had the usual birthday celebration. He started opening gifts and when he got to ours, he ripped open the box, threw the pair of pants on the floor and with a huge smile on his face said, "It's a box!" The rest of the day that was all he played with. Because he was so excited, we started to take photographs. He looked up, put his hand out as if to stop us, and said, "No pictures."

When Jake was five, he was in the backseat of the car with his mom and his aunt. His aunt was much more liberal in her thinking than the rest of the family. They were discussing religion and spirituality and Jake was listening. Finally he piped up and said, "Excuse me, Aunt Sally, but no one knows the mind of God!"

Pretty profound for a five-year-old.

Claudia Nelson

Claudia M. Nelson is the executive assistant to the chairman and CEO of The Stanley Works, a worldwide manufacturer and marketer of tools, hardware, and specialty hardware products. She has published numerous professional articles and poems.

IT'S IN THE GENES

*H*aving a grandchild (and entire family) 1,800 miles away is hard, so every holiday I make the journey from Connecticut to Wisconsin to see everyone. On July 3,

2003, I finally arrive at my daughter Anita's home in Milwaukee. Halfway up the walk I see her and my granddaughter, Natalie, coming down the other end of the walk to meet me.

They have just returned—Anita from the doctor (she's having twins!) and two-year-old Natalie from the babysitter. It's apparent that on this hot, summer day she has been swimming. Her hair is plastered down, and she's running happily toward me, shirt off and shorts in a half-dry condition.

"Oh, Natalie! Did you have fun in the pool?" I ask.

"That's not water," my daughter responds wearily.

It seems the "Energizer Bunny" (as we sometimes call her) started a Vaseline fight with the babysitter's young son. She won, but you would never know it from the quantity of Vaseline in this child's hair.

We spend the next several hours trying to clean her hair; the hardest part is the greased pig syndrome as she slips away from us when we try to hold her.

Finally, in utter frustration, I call my mother: the cleaning woman of all cleaning women. My mother uses the more unconventional methods of cleaning—no Windex for her! It's all baking soda, newspapers, ammonia, and vinegar. Sure enough, she tells me to use vinegar.

We try it—and Natalie's hair comes out glossy! I call my mother back to let her know it worked.

"Mom, it worked like a charm! I think this is so funny: Anita did the same thing when she was two!"

Then came the words every grandmother hates to hear from great-grandma.

"So did you." She laughs.

Vaseline fighting runs in the family. Who would have guessed?

Grandparents and grandchildren are a celebration of perfection and nurturing love.

—PRESIDENT JIMMY CARTER

Randy Neugebauer

Randy Neugebauer is a United States representative from the 19th District of Texas. His experience in business prior to his election has helped him serve on the House Committees on Agriculture, Science, and Resources.

DOUGHNUT FRIDAY

Several years ago, I started a tradition with my two grandsons, Nate and Noah, called "Doughnut Friday." The motive was to initiate an opportunity to spend time with them on a consistent basis.

So every Friday, my wife, Dana, and I would get up

and go to the local doughnut store and get a dozen or so doughnuts and head for their house. Most of the time we would be met by two very anxious young men, both vying to carry the box to the kitchen table. It became a great family time, as we were always joined by their parents, my son and daughter-in-law.

It also was teaching time; the boys learned the days of the week at an early age and knew that when they went to bed on Thursday night, tomorrow would be "Doughnut Friday." They learned about expressing their preferences, as each has his favorite flavor. Additionally, they learned to count and would tell me how many they had eaten or how many were left.

We also discussed manners and we had a rule that you only put one doughnut at a time on your plate. This kept all the doughnuts from becoming sampled doughnuts. If one brother was tempted to get more than one, the other brother reminded him quickly "one at a time." Now that I am in Congress and not living in the same city, the tradition continues with their mom and dad, and on occasions when I am home, we still celebrate "Doughnut Friday."

And by the way, besides loving my two grandsons, I love doughnuts, too.

❧ ❧

Hugh Ogden

Hugh Ogden is an award-winning poet and a professor of English and Poetry at Trinity College in Hartford, Connecticut. He is the author of five books of poetry and was nominated for the Pushcart Prize in 1998.

ROARING BROOK: HER CHRISTENING

(for my granddaughter, Amelia Ruth)

Talk about curving when the Reverend
bent over to touch a palm to her fore-
head, reached out in a human arc
and splashed water over her white
pinafore, spoke as he curved with
his cupped hand dripping brook-water
that runs church-side down through
Cotton Hollow, said what flows from
gravity welcomes the newborn into
the community and carries the centuries
into a sun-washed Sunday morning and
if you believe or don't these are

still waters from which life comes,
still the future in which the past
pours through a glacial-carved gap
of mill ruins, washing over our lives.

Children's children are the crown of old men.

—PROVERBS 17:6

George Olah

George A. Olah is the Distinguished Professor and Donald P. and Katherine B. Loker Chair in Organic Chemistry at the University of Southern California. He was awarded the Nobel Prize in 1994 for his contribution to carbocation chemistry.

*H*aving grandchildren is a great blessing and a wonderful experience. We have three: Peter, Kaitlyn, and Justin. It is only when becoming grandparents that you realize all the pleasures that your grandchildren give you, without most of the responsibilities and worries you had while bringing up your children. We have two great sons, George and Ron, and our delightful daughters-in-law, Sally and Cindy. The parents' responsibility is to take care of the grandchildren. Including, at the end of a visit, taking them home allowing you to relax, keeping the nice memories. Probably you will be closer to collapsing and going to bed after having tried to keep up with their unlimited energies. It is also perfectly permissible to spoil your grandchildren and leave disciplining to their parents (who, if I remember well, just a little while ago strongly objected to any such effort). What a pleasant change and great blessing it is to be grandparents.

It is, of course, not possible to have grandchildren first. My wife (a wonderful grandmother to whom I have been married for fifty-four years) and I frequently wonder, how did we manage the energy needed to bring up our two sons, in addition to our professional life, home duties, and so many other things. Of course, when you are young you don't appreciate many things and take them for granted. George Bernard Shaw, a long time ago, said that youth is wasted on the young, or at least the young do not fully appreciate their blessings. I don't really complain, however, because we have a wonderful family and gladly would start all over again, maybe a little wiser and appreciative of our blessings.

                             ❧ ❧

James Orr

James F. Orr is Chairman and CEO of Convergys Corporation.

SAMMY AND THE CEO

In thinking of the wonder of grandchildren, I could fill a book with all they represent, but for the purposes of this book, I will use this little anecdote as a reflection of how the hearts and spirits of grandchildren move the hearts and spirits of grandparents in a way that's hard to imagine before these wonderful little people enter your life. We have three beautiful grandchildren and a fourth on the way. I could talk with equal joy about any one of them, but the incident I'd like to share is one where a two-and-a-half-year-old granddaughter not only melted her Poppy's heart, but also stared down a CEO.

After a long and snowy winter, my wife, Cathy, suggested it was time to move the ficus trees from the sunny loggia in our breakfast room to their rightful and intended place at the far corners of our screened porch and dutifully, I did. But like all sun-starved living things, over the winter their reach for the sun had left them lush on one side and bare on the other. However, once back in their home at the far corner of the screened porch, their uneven growth with one naked side made them look decidedly unattractive, not to mention their height, which now obscured the sconces intended to light the porch.

Conscientiously, I decided for their own appearance and well-being, and for the benefit of those needing light on the porch, I would prune and shape them, as well as provide the appropriate nutrition to encourage lush growth. Having done that, I retired to my study to deal with other equally weighty matters. Less than thirty minutes later, my deliberations were disturbed by the very noticeable thumping of small but emphatic feet headed in my direction. I prepared to greet my granddaughter, Sammy (Samantha), when much to my surprise she appeared with her right index finger extended pointedly at me. This caused me some concern, because it carried with it an accusatorial tone. "Poppy," she said, "don't you cut Grammy's trees; you made a mess." For emphasis, having completed this unexpected dressing down, she then folded her arms across her chest and put out her bottom lip in a decidedly Shirley Temple-like demonstration of disapproval.

My wife had entered my study just before the final act in this comic tragedy and, despite her clear annoyance with me, it was all we could both do to keep from laughing. Sammy had certainly put me in my place and delivered an emphatic message I won't soon forget.

Apparently Sammy was present on the porch when Cathy discovered my horticultural handiwork and was expressing her anger at my "involvement in her business." Having absorbed this, I suspect with some encouragement, Sammy embarked on her mission to "set me straight."

It's an incident that Cathy and I will long and fondly remember, not for the specifics of its origin, but for the spunk and personality of our wonderful granddaughter. She was and is, as are our other grandchildren, Carson and Gwyneth, a wonder to behold.

There are fathers who do not love their children; there is no grandfather who does not adore his grandson.

—VICTOR HUGO

Solomon Ortiz

Solomon P. Ortiz is a United States representative from the 27th District of Texas. He has been a member of the House since 1982. He is a member of the House Armed Services Committee and the House Resources Committee.

I fell in love with my grandson, Oscar, much the same way I fell in love with my children when they were born. But grandchildren are different. Children fight with their parents and cuddle with their grandparents; grandparents have a much better deal.

This little guy can bend me to his will with one look or the touch of his little hand grabbing one of my fingers. He makes me think more about the future and what his role in it will be. I see all the members of my family in his face, in his mannerisms.

Oscar has a tremendous influence over me, and his very presence evokes a wide range of emotions. He makes me laugh. He makes me remember how hard it was to raise his parents, over twenty years ago. He makes me wonder what he will do with his life . . . where he will go to school . . . what job he will want to do . . . where he will travel on this earth. I thank God each time I see him and reflect on the wonder of birth, family, and future.

He's so smart. There's no telling how far he will go in his journey through life.

And his grandfather will be there as long as there is life in my body to cheer him on and be there as his helpmate, his confidant, and his champion.

Leon Panetta

Leon Panetta served as White House Chief of Staff under President Bill Clinton. He and his wife, Sylvia, are the founders and directors of The Panetta Institute, a nonpartisan center for the study of public policy located at California State University, Monterey Bay, California.

*W*e have three grandchildren. Two are Michael and Elizabeth, by our son Carmelo and his wife, Christina, and we have another Michael, Michael Leon (named after me), from our son Chris and his wife, Elizabeth.

This story involves little Michael Leon, who is only five years old. In Italian, grandfather is called "Nono" and grandmother is called "Nona." Michael calls my wife and me by those names. I had the honor of being asked to throw out the first pitch at a San Francisco Giants baseball game during the summer of 2003. Of course, I invited little Michael to come with me to the game and see me throw out the first pitch. We play catch together and he loves baseball, so I thought it'd be a real treat. His mother brought him to the game and as they were going through the turnstile, the ticket-taker looked down at little Michael (with his Giants hat and baseball glove) and said, "Who's your favorite baseball player?" expecting that Michael would answer, "Barry Bonds." Michael looked up with an expression of great pride and said, "My nono." The ticket-taker looked at his mom and asked, "Is that a new Japanese player?" Elizabeth replied, "No, that's his grandfather."

James Parkel

James G. Parkel was named president of the American Association of Retired Persons (AARP) in 2002. Previously, he was an executive with IBM for thirty-two years.

The average age of a first-time grandparent is forty-seven years. Forty-seven! That seems so young.

And it is. If you're forty-seven today, you can expect to live another thirty years. One hundred years ago that would have been the length of your entire life.

That shows just how much the landscape of aging has changed, although the collective mythology seems frozen in time: grandmothers wear flowery dresses and sensible shoes; grandfathers have flowing white beards and sit on rocking chairs. Yet, as every manufacturer of athletic goods knows, older people today are more likely to be run-ning in sneakers than sitting in rockers.

As the president of AARP, an association for those over fifty, I also know that today's grandparents are nothing like the old stereotypes. Some 75 percent of our 35 million mem-bers are grandparents and they are a very "un-retiring" group. According to our research and figures from the 2000 U.S. Census:

* Many grandparents work—53 percent work full time and 30 percent have not yet retired.
* There are more than 60 million grandparents in the United States.
* About 4.5 million grandparents in this country have primary responsibility for raising their grandchildren.
* Grandparents spend over $30 billion a year on their grandkids, dining out, going to movies, taking them on trips.

But none of that has any bearing on what it actually feels like to be a grandparent. And I can speak about that from personal experience.

The story begins with the relationship I had with my own grandparents. I grew up in the little town of Winslow, Arizona, right on the border of a Navajo Indian reservation. From the Navajos I learned the term *Hozho*, or *Blessing-way*. It means harmony, beauty, peace of mind, goodness, and health.

My grandfather was a fire-and-brimstone primitive Baptist preacher, but he and my grandmother lived in *Hozho*. They were warm, loving, had enormous inner strength, and had something kind to say about everybody.

In the summers, we would visit them at their farm in California. It was a small farm, but in my eyes it was heaven: a safe, warm place where I got to play with all my cousins. And there were plenty—my grandparents had twelve children, one of whom was my mother.

Later, as a callow, brash marine stationed in California, I'd invite my buddies to spend weekends at my grandparents' farm. We were always welcome. And oh, the farm-fresh food—especially the green beans. Good food. Warmth. R&R. Those were the pleasures that made spending time on my grandparents' farm so special.

Those experiences are like money in the bank—it's there to draw on whenever I need it. And over the years, I have needed it.

Today I am the proud grandfather of three who live in Austin, Texas, with my daughter and her husband. My daughter and I went through some hard years during her adolescence. I can truthfully say that now we understand each other just fine. The turning point came when she had her own children and I became a grandfather.

The first thing I learned was to keep my mouth shut. This is a lesson most grandparents figure out pretty soon. Parents are going to raise their kids in their own way.

And that's good. The way I look at it, I spent more than twenty years teaching my kids how to be parents. It's a relief not to have to give them on-the-job training today. It's also a relief not to have to scold or criticize my grandkids "for their own sake" in an effort to turn them into responsible human beings (though they do follow my rules when they're at my house). All I have to do is love them unconditionally. And that's easy.

In many ways, I guess our family is a typical blended American family. Three years ago I married a woman with two teenage children of her own. We all live together along with my teenage son. I'm also the grandparent of my daughter's teenage daughter. But there's no awkwardness among the generations. Although my daughter and her family live in Texas and we're in Connecticut, our two families are very close. We keep in touch through frequent visits and by phone. My grandkids especially like to call to share good news—like when my granddaughter made the golf team, or her sister became a cheerleader.

While grandparenting is one of the great joys of my life, it wasn't always so easy. I still recall one memorable weekend when my grandkids were much younger. I went down to Austin to take care of them for a weekend while my daughter and son-in-law went away to spend some time together. Here I was, a tough marine (so I thought), someone who could handle anything. When I arrived, the baby had the flu, which meant hourly diaper changes. Saturday we were closeted in the house all day—along with the four dogs and seven goldfish. I have never been so exhausted in my life, and that includes basic training.

The next day I decided it was time for an outing. We would surprise their parents with a new TV set. We all piled into the car to set off for some comparison shopping. Pretty soon they grew hungry and restless. I was ready to buy anything. Still, we ended up with a pretty nice TV. We drove home and got it connected. I was wiped out. The children fell into bed.

I was determined that my daughter and her husband would return to a quiet, clean, calm house. So I tidied up, poured myself a cool drink, and waited for them to return.

"How did you do it?" they asked, astonished. "It was nothing," I replied. "Won't you stay the night?" they asked. "No," I answered, "I don't think so." I was off on the first plane.

My grandchildren are such a joy to me because I am just the loving backstop in their upbringing. The pressure of being a primary caretaker is off. I get to just relax and enjoy them. It's almost as though the genes skipped a generation, and we are as compatible as pie.

By contrast, young parents are into their own lives, their own careers, their own marital struggles. By the time you're a grandparent, you not only know that the most priceless thing in life is love, you have the luxury of showering it all on your children's kids. And the older you get, the less judgmental, the less perfectionist, the more tolerant, the more forgiving. So while your relationship with your own children may still have a bit of an edge, with grandchildren, the decks are clear.

Grandparents I know feel the same way—just watch them pull out the latest photos of their grandkids. Research shows again and again that grandparents contribute significantly to the healthy development of their grandchildren.

I know that was the case with my own grandparents. And I hope one day my grandchildren will say the same about me.

～ ～

Willard on Great Lessons My Grandparents Taught Me

. . . . . .

Sometimes you don't have to do anything with your grandparents (or grandchildren); just being there is enough.

Family is the glue that holds the universe together.

The value of a dollar has changed since their day. It will probably continue to change in mine.

Human society always progresses, technologically and socially. Every generation helps to advance the next.

Times and trends, fads and friends: They all change; family is forever.

Bill Pascrell

Bill Pascrell, Jr., is a United States representative from the 8th Congressional District of New Jersey, a position he has held since 1996. He is a member of the House Select Committee on Homeland Security.

$\mathcal{M}$egan is my five-year-old granddaughter. She is a pistol. Mischief follows her. She tries to emulate everything her two older brothers do and causes an uproar with the least amount of effort. In the past year, one incident in particular comes to mind. My daughter-in-law, Kelly, and another member of the family went to visit her late mother and father's graves at the cemetery. Megan tagged along. At the sites, Kelly prayed for her deceased parents, referring to them in a soft voice as "Mom" and "Pop." That happens to be how Megan and her brothers refer to me— "Pop" and "Pop-pop." You see it coming, don't you?

A few days later, Megan was in school and the students in her class were asked to pray for a "loved one." When it came to Megan's turn, she clearly and succinctly turned to her classmates and then to her teacher and said, "I want us to pray for my Pop-Pop who died." Her classmates accepted but the teacher knew only one Pop-Pop for Megan and that was me, the congressman. She was shocked and immediately upon praying started to inquire as to why she hadn't heard about my death. The buzz went through the school and sure enough Kelly showed up at the end of the school day to fetch Megan and her brothers. Kelly was her usual bubbly self and for sure folks wondered, "Why the glee? After all, Pop-Pop is gone." Well, it was a bit premature, as Kelly was called on to clear the air and go to the source of the misunderstanding. "Yes, Mom, I told the class Pop-Pop died and we prayed." Kelly hugged her, everyone smiled, some even with relief. When Kelly called me that day, I almost collapsed with laughter. Kids really do say the darnedest things and thus innocence is so precious. This "Pop" lives on to hopefully watch his grandchildren grow and grow.

Noel Porter

Noel Porter is the maternal grandmother of Jesse Bradford, an actor who has appeared in King of the Hill *and* Romeo + Juliet, *following his television commercial debut at the age of eight months.*

*W*hen my grandson was about six or seven years old, he did something both simple and ingenious that I will never forget. I was making a peanut butter and jelly sandwich, a dish that I'd had over fifty years to refine. I had already spread peanut butter on one piece of bread, and, customarily, I was beginning to add the jelly on top. As always, it was proving sloppy and difficult to spread the jelly onto the peanut butter, when suddenly Jesse piped up, "Nana, why don't you put the jelly on the other piece of bread so it's not all messy."

I don't know how in fifty years I never came up with that on my own, but it's been a time saver and an oft-told story of my grandson's brilliance (not to mention of an admiring grandmother's love) ever since.

Harve Presnell

Harve Presnell is an actor who has appeared in many stage and film productions, including such blockbusters as Fargo *(1996) and* Saving Private Ryan *(1998).*

You would think, out of an even dozen,
There would be a like-pair;
Not a chance.
Just twelve extraordinarily unique, marvelously gifted
Wonderfuls to look at: six boys, six girls . . .
Our Grandchildren.
Absolute order out of random selection
To be known as
Big Dad and Gammy
Or
Dub and Gummy
Beats the hell out of
PawPaw and Poopy
Or
Noonie and Nummie
Anyday!

On behalf of and in order of appearance Chet Michael (twenty-two), Caylen (nineteen), Janai (sixteen), Kirk Shane (sixteen), Emma Claire (fifteen), Rose Claire (fourteen), Morgan Rose (thirteen), Garrick Nevar (thirteen), Kyra Shea (ten), Isabeau Alora (nine), Sean Larkin (nine), and (from the Ukraine) Carmina Elise (four) . . . I am subjectively their

Dub and/or Big Dad . . . formally known as
Harve Presnell

Cliff Robertson

Cliff Robertson is an actor who has appeared in a wide variety of films, often as supporting characters. He was personally selected to play a young JFK by the president himself, in PT 109 *(1963), a movie about young Kennedy's experiences in World War II.*

I knew I was in trouble—indeed I had been forewarned years ago—that grandchildren were a new dimension. Dimension—hell, a new world! However, I was not prepared when my three-and-a-half-year-old, Cynthia Jackson, running around the outdoor swimming pool in Charleston, South Carolina, was warned by her mother, my daughter Stephanie, in the following dialogue, "Careful, darling. Don't run too fast. You don't want to trip and fall."

Cinnie continues running.

A moment later, her mother again warns, "Careful, sweetheart, not too fast."

A moment later, "Cinnie, be careful darling—be careful!"

The little three-and-a-half-year-old towhead stopped, turned to her mother, and with a philosophical sigh said, "Mom, it happens."

Her "get-a-life" tone was enough to shut all the adults nearby to a stunned silence, including this grandfather, who looks forward to her sage advice as we both grow older.

Ned Rorem

Ned Rorem is a composer and author. He was awarded the 1976 Pulitzer Prize in music and was named "the world's best composer of art songs" by Time *magazine.*

Because I am gay, I have no biological grandchildren. However, I am a grand-uncle eleven times over.

For the record, these eleven young people form a rainbow coalition: my dear sister Rosemary's WASP children having spouses who are Black, Jewish, and Asian.

My chief pleasure in these relationships is that I have much admiration and little responsibility.

Neil Sedaka

Neil Sedaka is a singer, songwriter, and performer who has brought the American public such classic hits as "Breaking Up Is Hard To Do" (1962) and "Calendar Girl" (1961).

On January 29 of 2003, we were doubly blessed with the arrival of our twin granddaughters, Amanda Esther and Charlotte Dawn. I was performing in Las Vegas when my wife, Leba, called with the news. The thrill of announcing to the audience that I was a grandfather was something I had been waiting many years to do.

The girls are seven months at this writing, and their individual personalities are becoming quite evident. Amanda is the musician. She seems to perk up when she hears her "Papa" singing (her favorite is "Laughter in the Rain"). She also is quite a hand at the Step & Play, although she plays it with her feet. Charlotte is more into Elmo and Big Bird, but I'm not giving up.

I can't wait to take them to the park, the movies, have long talks with them, teach them the piano, and make sure they know their Papa loves them very much, and he and Nana will always be there for whatever they need. Isn't that our job?

Bernie Siegel

Bernie Siegel, M.D., is perhaps best known for his book
Love, Medicine, and Miracles: Lessons Learned about
Self-Healing from a Surgeon's Experience with Excep-
tional Patients. *Dr. Siegel is a supporter of charities that
help the children and animals of the world who, as he puts it,
"can't speak for themselves, but are more complete than we
adults are. They live in their hearts, not in their heads."*

WHY ARE THEY CALLED GRANDCHILDREN?

I must share two experiences with you that make me feel
no one should have children until they are at least sixty. I
was born an ugly duckling. My mother had a serious med-
ical problem and was advised not to become pregnant. She
did anyway and when her labor went on for days, and she
was not a candidate for a cesarean section due to her med-
ical problem, I was finally dragged out. She said, "I wasn't
handed a baby; I was handed a purple melon. Your father
wrapped you in a kerchief and I put you in a carriage, covered it, and placed it at the back of the house so you
wouldn't upset anybody."

If I had been left there, I can tell you from research on

newborns of every species that I would very likely be an addict, chronically and seriously ill today, or dead. So what happened? I had a grandmother who took me out of the carriage, oiled my head and body, and began massaging me, "pushing everything back where it belonged," to again quote my mother.

When I was reading *The Ugly Duckling* to our grand-children, I realized how fortunate I was. The Ugly Duck-ling did what most of us cannot achieve on our own. He was thrown out of his home by an unwed mother and was still able to recognize his beauty reflected back at him by an inanimate mirror. On the other hand, I didn't have to prove anything or struggle to realize I was a swan; I had a grandmother who could accept me unconditionally and show me in her eyes and by her touch that I was a swan.

I practiced pediatric surgery for many years and cared for many children with various anomalies and birth de-fects. When our children were born, I felt that I needed to examine them as soon as they were born to be sure all the parts were there. The nurses thought there was something wrong with me and they were right. When I have been present at the birth of our grandchildren, I just wanted to hold and love them, not examine them. No matter what their problems may be, physical or emotional, they are our Grand Children and my job is to love them, not diagnose them. I may add that our children learned to say, "Dad, you're not in the operating room now," when I showed that aspect of my personality.

We all need role models to help us define ourselves and our actions. All I can say is when in doubt ask yourself, WWLGD, or "What would a loving grandparent do?" When some of the children I cared for were physically scarred or deformed, I just kept loving them and they came to realize that when you are loved, you are beautiful. Some of them made me their CG or "Chosen Grandfather"; others are health professionals themselves today, having learned that when you give love you can't be ugly except to those who don't understand.

So re-parent the grandchildren of the world and help them to develop the self-esteem, self-worth, and self-love that every child of God deserves. Become a CG and make a difference in someone's life. And when in doubt, remember, WWLGD!

Govern a family as you would cook a small fish— very gently.

—CHINESE PROVERB

Richard Simmons

Richard William Simmons starred as the title role in the hit series Sergeant Preston of the Yukon. *In the show, the Canadian Mountie Sergeant Preston fought crime with the help of his horse, Rex, and his dog, Yukon King. Mr. Simmons passed away on January 11, 2003. His wife, Billie Brown Simmons, contributed this essay, which he had written about his grandson, Todd.*

There he stood looking out the window at the blowing trees. Perhaps at his own reflection in the window. The sun and the trees created exciting shadows on the cement decking just beyond the window.

Todd Christopher Simmons, my grandson, age sixteen months, was strong, sturdy, and healthy. Possessed of a cheerful countenance and huge brown eyes that were set in his pixie face by his mother and God.

I sat behind him, a bare few feet, filled to overflowing with a grandfather's pride. I could almost imagine what was going on in the little mind of Todd. I was almost jealous. Such wonderful things happen in the minds of little children. Why does the wind blow? Why does a shadow move? Why can't I fly like a bird does?

Sometimes it seems a shame that they come to know the answers and then have to move to unanswerable things. What would life be like for Todd? This jungle of tall buildings and ribbons of concrete that lace our land?

Where would the tall grass be that a boy could lie in to watch the formations of white clouds become anything he could imagine them to be—castles, dragons, ships, and huge animals. Would there be a deserted train track to walk, or a dirt road to walk on in his bare feet?

Certainly no horse-drawn ice wagon to follow and get a good chunk of ice. A fellow could always wash it off in a puddle. Where would that old pump in some backyard be? The cold, clear water that tasted like cold, clear water.

The shortcut to a friend's house a mile or so away, through a tall cornfield. It was fun to get lost and eat raw corn off the cob. I'll feel sort of sad if he misses a green-apple bellyache.

He has to know the disappointment of losing his first kite on a wire or a tree, or his best agate to a friend. I would like to be there to see the bloody rag wrapped around a stubbed toe. To know of his secret hiding place for a slightly used wad of gum, or other goodies he couldn't quite finish. I had one. Mine was an old Civil War statue that stood in the park across the street. Up on the second pedestal just under his left boot. No girl could climb that high.

What would it be worth to see him singing in the

church choir on Easter Sunday with his first black eye? I would like to see him lug his sack on his daily paper route. Roll the paper and peg it thirty feet to and on a front porch.

To walk in the rain and get soaking wet only to have his mother give him a "you know what" for being so foolish. But it was worth it. What did mothers know about walking in the rain and getting soaking wet?

There is no feeling in the world like bringing home your first stray dog. I hope he can think of a million reasons why he should keep him. 'Cause good stray dogs are hard to find. Especially with fleas.

A grandson is a promise of tomorrow. He makes a man stand tall in his own image. Self-glorifying? I don't believe so. Satisfaction? Perhaps in a way, but more than anything else, I believe there stand the fruits of your efforts in your own son. To watch your own son love Todd, protect him, play with him, to reflect with pride in what God has given him.

As we used to say when we were kids, "If you had one wish, what would you wish for?" I would take Todd Christopher back to White Bear Lake, Minnesota, where I lived and show him the cornfields, the ice wagons, and the place where I used to hide my slightly used wad of gum.

ॐ ॐ

Paul Simon

Paul Simon served as United States senator from Illinois. He was also a professor at Southern Illinois University and founder and director of the university's Public Policy Institute. He passed away on December 9, 2003.

*W*illard Scott is correct. Grandchildren are great!

I have four: three granddaughters—Reilly, Brennan, and C. J.—and one grandson, Nick. They range in age from seven to thirteen.

Not only are they fun, they are a way to measure the progress of our society. When my son and daughter were infants, changing those cloth diapers (which we washed) had to be done with safety pins, and there was always the concern that you might stick one of them if he or she turned quickly, which they frequently did. And, of course, you could stick yourself.

It is marvelous to see grandchildren adapt to new things so easily. I am writing this on a manual typewriter, on which I write all my books and articles. I do research on the computer, but it is still a strange beast to me—but not to my grandchildren.

I believe that we're the only nation in the world in

which all elementary students do not study another language. Approximately 7 percent of our grade school pupils do now, up from one percent three decades ago, but still abysmal. I didn't learn another language in grade school, nor did my children. But my children and their spouses are creating that opportunity for my grandchildren. They all speak a little Spanish, and in the summer, two of my granddaughters went to a Japanese language camp for two weeks. It will help them in ways I cannot gauge, and it will help to create a world of a little greater understanding.

When I grew up, there were no Little Leagues to play baseball or any sport. My son had that opportunity, but not my daughter. Now there are organized sports teams available for both girls and boys, and on those rare occasions that I get to see one of my grandchildren play, it is more fun than any major league contest.

Those youngsters learn how to play and also learn sportsmanship. If only we could teach that to some of their parents and grandparents!

❦ ❦

Nancy Sinatra

Nancy Sinatra was the first wife of legendary musician and actor Frank Sinatra.

I've heard that expression—"If I had known grandchildren were so much fun, I would have had them first"—time and again over the years. I don't know who said it first but I've said it myself and it's certainly true.

Just kidding, of course.

I love my children with all of my heart, but nothing can beat my grandkids.

William Jay Smith

William Jay Smith is a poet who served as Consultant in Poetry to the Library of Congress from 1968 until 1970. Today, this position is known as the United States Poet Laureate.

WHAT IS AIR?

On a cold day in the country my four-year-old grandson Alex was helping me build a fire in a stove set on the hearth of an old fireplace we no longer used.

I lifted the damper.

"Why are you doing that?" he asked.

"To let out the smoke and let in some air," I answered.

"What is air?" he asked.

And indeed what a question! I hesitated, knowing that no dictionary definition would do. The one I found later, "a colorless, odorless, tasteless, gaseous mixture mainly nitrogen and oxygen," would certainly have left him even more in the dark than he'd previously been.

"Air," I said finally, "is what surrounds us, what we breathe, what gives us life."

I was not at all satisfied with my response, but it seemed to satisfy Alex. He moved on at once to another difficult, if not impossible, question.

Later I realized that I should have answered him immediately with a riddle, as someone centuries ago may have done when asked the same question:

> *A house full, a hole full,*
> *And you cannot gather a bowl full.*

The answer to this, given usually as "smoke," may also be "air," and was clearly the ageless imaginative answer I'd been seeking.

When a little older, Alex would relish such riddles, which spring from the very base of the language with which he was now constantly toying. He confidently displayed later that day an ever-growing mastery of it when he emitted a resounding bit of utter nonsense, then paused, and added proudly, "I'm almost talking," meaning, of course, that he was perfectly capable of speaking properly if he'd chosen to do so.

He was not only learning our language, but, playing with it, had become a conscious explorer off to examine, as he had already been doing for several years, every minute piece of that vast territory.

Alex is now a twenty-one-year-old junior in college. One day he may have grandchildren of his own who will put to him the same questions that he once put to me, questions that will recall for him, as they had for me, those early years that offer every one of us a good portion of the world's wonder.

Carroll Spinney

Carroll Spinney is a puppeteer who is perhaps best known for his role as Big Bird on Sesame Street.

When my first grandchild, Wyatt, was six months old, he fell in love with Big Bird. His first words were not "Mommy" or "Daddy," but "Bub-bub." As he grew older and we were talking on the phone, I would put Big Bird on the phone to talk to him. Big Bird and Wyatt had a wonderful relationship. He would talk to Big Bird more freely than he would to me. He would tell Big Bird things he wouldn't tell me.

When he was about eleven, he found out who Big Bird really was. I suppose the disappointment was similar to that of a child finding out the truth about Santa; at least Big Bird was played by his grandfather! I will always miss the days of Big Bird and his own little friend on the phone.

Dear Grandmamma, with what we give,
We humbly pray that you may live

For many, many happy years:
Although you bore us all to tears.

—HILAIRE BELLOC

Maureen Stapleton

Maureen Stapleton is an actress who got her start on the stage. Her performance on Broadway in the Tennessee Williams play The Rose Tattoo *earned her a Tony Award. She went on to star on the silver screen, winning an Academy Award for her portrayal of Emma Goldman in the 1981 classic film* Reds.

I love my grandchildren!

Thomas Sullivan

Thomas C. Sullivan is a former chairman and CEO of RPM International, Inc., a holding company that owns subsidiaries that deal in specialty coatings.

*W*hen my father passed away, on August 18, 1971, I became chairman and CEO of the firm he started in 1947, which at the time was an $11 million company traded on the over-the-counter market. When I retired this past October, RPM, Inc. was a $2 billion New York Stock Exchange company and my son Frank C. Sullivan, named after my father, took over as CEO. On July 28, 2003, he announced RPM's all-time record earnings at the NYSE, and the opening bell that day was rung in by his son, Frank C. Sullivan III ("Sully"), both of whom were standing under the flag. Sully is the oldest of our fourteen grandchildren—it doesn't get any better than that!

Terri Tepper and Lawrence Weiner

Terri Tepper is a portrait photographer, educator, speaker, and coauthor of The New Entrepreneurs: Women Working From Home. *She also founded the Center for a Woman's Own Name and the Consumer Credit Project, a private enforcement agency on women's credit rights.*

Lawrence Weiner is a lawyer and former Department of Justice federal prosecutor. An elected member of the Illinois

State Bar Association's General Assembly, he is active in several community organizations including the Harvard Law School mentor program for disadvantaged Chicago youth.

This married couple was inducted into the Grandparents of America Hall of Fame in 2003.

FIRST GRANDCHILD:
WILL FLY, WEEKLY

I was ready to be a grandma as soon as our daughter got married, but I realized two things: 1) She and our son-in-law lived a plane ride away, and 2) she was focused on the career for which her schooling prepared her. She was on the partnership track of a large consulting firm. Grandchildren were not on the horizon. One day, our daughter called to tell us she was pregnant.

Soon after, while vacationing together, the issue of childcare came up since Nona planned on continuing to work. I don't recall exactly how the idea surfaced, but my being the baby's nanny despite the distance seemed viable. My husband, Lawre, was all for it right from the start. Still, all sorts of issues had to be addressed. A third realization hit me: 3) The way to the grandchildren is through the parents. In my mind, I envisioned myself bathing the baby and presenting him or her to the happy parents upon their return from a hard day's work. "No," they said. They wanted to bathe their baby. It would be easier for me if I looked at nannying as a job, the description of which would be defined by the parents.

"We'll pay the airfare," my daughter told me. "You're really doing us a favor. No amount of money could pay for the kind of loving care you'll be giving our baby. Besides, you're actually saving us money. The cost of the airfare is cheaper than a full-time nanny."

"Do you have any requirements of us?" they asked me.

"If I come four days a week," I said, "I'd like you, Nona, to be there on Fridays. I want the baby coming to you, not to me." And she agreed. She was able to negotiate working from home on Fridays.

Months passed and we continued to work out issues. One day as we sat around our small round kitchen table, Tom and Nona addressed my request that if anything happened to them, we'd like to be guardians of the baby. It seemed so obvious to me since I already would be such a big part of the baby's life. And what's more, Lawre and I had asked my parents to be our children's guardians. It felt like the beginning of a precedent.

"Terri," Tom said, "we're not going to make you and Lawre guardians of this baby or future children. I don't want to offend you, but you're sixty now. By the time our baby is a teenager you'll be in your seventies. If we have other children you could be in your eighties."

I felt healthy. I couldn't see any reason why my husband and I wouldn't be sufficiently fit to take care of one or more teenagers. I had been a teacher and taught them. I'm sure my face got very red. I could feel it and the sweat running down my back. I felt conflicted. I wanted so much to be this baby's nanny and I didn't want anything to stand in the way.

I didn't sleep well that night. Not until morning was I able to attach a word to the intensity of my feelings. I said to Lawre, "You know what? I'm in a rage!"

"I don't blame you," he said. "That was tough to take."

Behind my rage was the bitterness of seeing our first grandchild retreat into whatever family Nona and Tom chose to become his or her guardians. I had read about grandparents who had limited access to their grandchildren. I felt it would be a certainty.

Even now I wonder about co-guardianship with Lawre and if we will be consulted when problems or difficult decisions come up, in case we have something to offer. Back then, I didn't understand why age should be a more important criterion than love. After all, grandparental love is a very special kind of love with the unique perspective of having already dealt with, and learned from, growing-up issues and their consequences. I realized, however, that I needed to concentrate not on what was remotely possible, but what was likely to happen in the near future. I wanted to get to know our first grandchild. That was my number one priority.

Nona and I walked around the community lake. She told me she'd like me with her the week before the due date. She'd take off work so we could spend time together. And, although she wanted only Tom in the delivery room, she wanted me there during labor and after the birth. Tom was in agreement. What a lovely gift that was. The passion of the guardianship issue began to fade. Nona went on to mention that she and Tom wanted to be alone with their new baby soon after they had come home from the hospital, and Lawre had flown out to see the baby. Of course, I understood and I appreciated their candidness.

I certainly didn't want to be intrusive and so thought about a bed-and-breakfast on a weekly basis, but I couldn't find a convenient one. Nona said she'd love to have me stay at the house. I thought about how intense Nona's work was with meetings that sometimes caused her to miss taking an earlier train home. The same was true of Tom as a doctor and part of the staff at a leading big city teaching hospital. I could make it a little easier for them by being available when they had to work late.

Laura was born November 17, 2000. For thirteen months, starting in March 2001 when our daughter went back to work, I commuted from Chicago to the East Coast. I left on Sunday evenings until the tragedy of 9/11, after which I left on Monday afternoons and returned on Thursdays. My mother recognized the stress I was beginning to show and insisted I cut back a day. Our son, Jordan, stepped up to drive me to the airport on Mondays, and Nona found a nanny replacement for that day.

We worked out problems when they arose. Nona's job involved national travel, and since she was breast-feeding, I went with her. I'd take the baby to the zoo or seek out friends in that city during the day. Back on the East Coast, I exposed Laura to as many different environments as I could: aquariums, Mommy and Me classes, parks, petting zoos. I didn't want that baby to be afraid of animals.

I started reading to Laura as soon as she could sit up. I began teaching a Photographing Your Baby class at the local YWCA, bringing Laura with me to model. The mothers brought their babies to class, too. I would teach the women as they photographed their babies. We made heirloom ABC photographic books using family members to illustrate the letters of the alphabet. Besides being an educator, author, and speaker, I had been a professional photographer for twelve years. I brought every piece of my background experience with me to my nanny job.

I saw the development of a little person from infanthood to thirteen months and I saw it in a way I never seemed to have had time for when raising our own children. Nona and Tom have since had twin daughters, and Nona did make partner that year I helped her. Nona asked me if and how much I'd like to be involved with the twins. Tom was right—I didn't have the energy I anticipated I'd have. I gave them a month of help over the summer and now we visit every six weeks for a three-day weekend.

There was no greater gift Nona and Tom could have given me than sharing their first baby in such a personal way. On a recent visit, as we said good-bye, Laura, almost three, kissed Papa Lawre and insisted on hugging him. Then she folded herself into my arms and lay there limply, her head resting on my shoulder. Neither of us said anything for a long time. Minutes passed. I said softly, "Don't you want to finish the story you were reading with your friend?" She gave me one more kiss and then ran back upstairs.

 $\mathcal{M}$ y grandchildren have inspired my imagination to write poems, books, and stories that will enhance our bonding and hopefully provide enjoyment for them and other grandchildren. My "Hello Book" and "Laura and the Duck" story are just two examples of the many I have written.

HELLO BOOK

Hello Sun,
Your bright golden rays,
Warm us in so many ways.

Hello Clouds,
You fill the sky's spaces,
Full of animals and faces.

Hello Rain,
Your pitter patter to and fro,
Makes the flowers in the garden grow.

Hello Fog,
With your watery mist,
Hiding things that really exist.

Hello Snow,
Your white flakes and designs,
Enchant us during winter times.

Hello Moon,
So big and bright,
Your face shines upon my face at night.

Hello Stars,
Forever blinking,
To light the sky while we are sleeping.

© Lawrence Jay Weiner 2002

LAURA AND THE DUCK

One day Laura went to a pond and saw goldfish and ducks. A duck waddled up to Laura and said, "Quack." "What do you want?" said Laura. And the duck said, "Quack." Laura thought about this and figured out that the duck was hungry and wanted food. Laura gave the duck some corn. The duck said, "Quack." Laura knew that quack meant thank you.

❦ ❧

Laura had me read the duck story several times. It was a special moment.

Willard on Why Being a Grandparent Is Better Than Being a Parent

. . . . . .

You can do diapers on your own schedule.

You no longer wonder whether or not you were a good parent—you know that you are.

At the end of the day, when you're an exhausted grandparent, the kids go home.

You get to give presents when you want to.

You have more time to be there for your grandkids than you did as a parent.

For some inexplicable reason, you relate better to your grandchildren than you do to your children.

Through your grandkids you can witness the social changes between generations.

You get to watch your kids being parents.

When you have grandchildren, you have a sense of the persistence of the future: You understand the circle of life.

You can see family traits as they travel through the generations more than you could with your own children.

Craig Thomas

Craig Thomas is a United States senator from Wyoming and formerly served as United States representative. He is an outspoken advocate for rural America.

Grandchildren are great—what a wonderful addition they are! The best thing is that you can be there when there's a lot of fun going on, and when the work begins, you can suddenly have to go home.

It's also possible to divide them up so you only have to deal with one of them at a time. I don't know quite how you can handle that, but having grandchildren, rather than your own kids, sounds like a good deal. Actually, the most fun part is watching my kids be the parents. They do a great job. My grandkids are involved in so many more activities than anyone would have ever imagined. It's a busy life. There's nothing better than having a family including grandchildren. They are great!

Richard Thornburgh

Richard Thornburgh has held a variety of positions in government over the years, including governor of Pennsylvania, Attorney General (under two presidents), and a United Nations official.

CHILDREN AND GRANDCHILDREN— OUR BRIDGE TO THE FUTURE

$\mathcal{M}$ary Chapin Carpenter, in her lovely ballad "Halley Came to Jackson," sings of a father holding an infant in his arms as Halley's Comet streaked across the sky in Jackson, Mississippi, in 1910. On that night, he expresses the hope that the baby will be around seventy-six years hence for the next visit of this cosmic phenomenon—an event that does indeed come to pass—reminding us anew that life is a true continuum. This song never fails to bring a tear to my eye when I think of my own six grandchildren and their future in a world of constant challenge.

Our children and grandchildren are our personal bridges to the future. Long after our days on this earth have run their course, they will be obliged to take up the tasks we have left unfinished. Our principal task should be to equip them for that effort in positive ways—to help mold qualities of character, integrity, joy, and compassion, which can combine with a strong faith in their ability, with God's help, to create a better world.

It is not an assignment without reward. While it is often difficult to envision that those whom we cuddle on our laps or bounce on our knees today will be tomorrow's leaders, that is indeed what will come to pass in the fullness of time. Moreover, there is a particularly subtle gift that grandchildren give to us as grandparents. They are a constant reminder to their own parents—our children—of how very much we love them as they watch their own offspring grow to maturity.

Nowhere is that hoary adage that "what goes around comes around" more literally true than with our grandchildren. Just like Halley's Comet in the song, when our days have passed, our children's children will be there to face up to the same kinds of problems that we, their forebears, had to deal with. And, with God's help, they will excel where we have fallen short.

True, we are the bridge between the past and the present for our children and grandchildren but, more important, they are our bridge to the future—a future which they will build but we will not see.

Cecil Underwood

Cecil Underwood is the former governor of West Virginia. In 1957, he became the state's youngest governor and later served a second term in 1996.

A good friend, Marian McQuade of Oak Hill, West Virginia, was the founder of National Grandparents Day, which celebrated its twenty-fifth anniversary in 2003. She was the mother of fifteen children. I had a photograph taken with her and all her children in the Governor's Office during my first term. She was a very active civic and volunteer leader all her busy life. Willard Scott has focused much national attention on Grandparents Day through his television recognition of people who have reached the century birth date.

Willard came to the Greenbrier Hotel to deliver a breakfast speech to the annual West Virginia Business Summit on

September 4, 1998. I was honored to welcome him to West Virginia as he did his live telecast on the *Today* show from a horse-drawn carriage on the Greenbrier front lawn.

Two of our three children were born during my first term as governor, from 1957 to 1961. Our son Craig was born January 16, 1957, the second day I was governor. My wife, Hovah, spent inauguration night in the Governor's Mansion, then went to the hospital the next day. We named him Craig, a Celtic name meaning "rocky road." Our second daughter was born on January 15, 1959.

Each of our children has given us two grandchildren, ranging in age from four to nineteen years. Our son's two are the youngest, and they live in Boston; hence we don't get to see them very often, but we do communicate by telephone and e-mail.

Our two daughters and their families live in the Charleston area, so we are close to those four grandchildren. Our oldest grandson is now a freshman at West Virginia University, majoring in sports journalism and political science.

During my second term, from 1996 to 2001, all the grandchildren enjoyed visiting the Governor's Mansion, where they had plenty of room to play, explore, and make noise. The chefs and their staff paid special attention to the grandchildren and in the process spoiled them to think life would always be this good.

Our two oldest grandsons, Christopher and Coleman Richardson, accompanied us to all the National Governors'

Association summer conferences—Las Vegas, Milwaukee, St. Louis, and State College. They took full advantage of the excellent children's programs at each conference. They made solid friendships with other governors' children and have kept in touch by e-mail and correspondence.

The 1998 conference was held in Milwaukee. Our oldest granddaughter, Mary Baker, went with us to this event. The entertainment highlight that year was the annual National Circus Day Parade. Dr. Daniel Draper, who chaired the chemistry department at Bethany College when I was the college president, became a full-time staff member at the National Circus headquarters near Milwaukee. He gave us a personal tour of the massive circus exhibits as he explained the history and purpose of each one; it was like a seminar on circus culture in America and the world. Mary became attached to Michigan Governor John Engler's triplet daughters. They sat on the curb to watch the entire circus parade.

Our 2001 summer family vacation was at the Canaan Valley Resort State Park in the mountains of West Virginia. The exciting event of this week was all the family taking the grandchildren riding the high ski lift from the bottom to the top of the mountain and returning. We enjoyed watching the grandchildren's suspense, fright, and reaction to this first experience.

The grandchildren all enjoy visits to my family farm where I was reared. They are fascinated with this old house and its antique furnishings. One special attraction has always been the crank telephone on the dining room wall; in my early years, this telephone was part of a community line maintained by its subscribers but it is now nonworking. On one visit, our young grandson Coleman climbed on a chair to crank the old phone and do a make-believe conversation. He said, "Granddad, I think I will call God," and I explained it would be a long distance call but encouraged him to proceed. After cranking the phone, he said, "Hello God, I am Coleman Richardson, and I am at my grandfather's farm in case you need to find me." After a pause, he said, "Oh, you already knew that."

On another visit to our home in Huntington, Coleman explained to me all the reasons he feared the dark. Another relative from Canton, Ohio, and her children were also visiting. The children decided to sleep in their sleeping bags in a large bedroom next to the master bedroom while their parents slept in another room over the kitchen, which did not connect with the two other bedrooms. When Coleman awakened in the middle of night, he was concerned about where his mother was. He passed up the elevator and made his way down the steps, through the living and dining rooms, and up the steps to the other bedroom—all in total darkness. I asked him why he made this journey if he was so afraid of darkness. His reply: "Well, Granddad, I was looking for some light."

The next day, he didn't eat much at the dinner table and asked to be excused. His father excused him but warned him, "If I catch you in the candy dish, you will be in big trouble!" In a few minutes, Coleman came through the dining room with a mouth full of chocolates. His father immediately challenged him, "Son, what did I tell you?" Coleman's smiling reply, "You said I would be in big trouble if you caught me in the candy dish."

Hovah and I agree with Willard Scott that grandchildren are so much fun. We cherish every moment with them as we watch them grow through one stage and change to another.

Jerry Vale

Jerry Vale is a singer who had a pocket-full of chart-topping hits in the 1950s. His popularity has surged into today, as his songs are often heard in films such as GoodFellas *and* Casino.

I have a grandchild and he has been the greatest pleasure of my life. He is probably the greatest love of my life. He is the cutest, most loving grandchild that anyone could ever have and he is so much fun. I love him with all my heart; I think that you could probably say that of all the

things in my life that I have had, he is the greatest gift I
have ever received. I just love him tremendously.

Dick Van Patten

*Dick Van Patten is a former child actor who went on to star in
the television classics* Eight is Enough *and* Mama. *He has
appeared in over twenty Broadway productions since his debut at the age of seven. He has also been featured in such
movies as* Spaceballs.

I have three grandsons; they are one, seven, and ten years
old. The oldest is Duke, whose father is Vincent Van Patten, who used to be a wonderful tennis player, and his
other grandfather is Max Lerner, who was a great intellect
and writer.

As a result, Duke is very athletic and also very bright.
He is the president of his whole public school in Malibu
and number one on the soccer team. So he inherits both
skills from his father and his other grandfather.

My whole life now is watching them in awe as they
continue to impress me.

Dick Vitale

Dick Vitale is one of the most famous basketball commentators of all time. His classic phrase, "It's awesome, baby!" rings in the basketball season every year.

FATHER'S DAY A HIT WITH GRANDKIDS AT BALLPARK

June 16, 2003

There is nothing like the national pastime, especially on Father's Day! Take me out to the ballgame, take me out to the crowd!

I had the time of my life on Sunday. Talk about a great Father's Day—there is nothing greater than this, as I was accompanied by my daughters, Sherri and Terri, to the Pirates-Devil Rays game. It was Fun City. I got there an hour before game time, and it was special because it marked the first game attended by my granddaughter Sydney and twin grandsons Connor and Jake.

It is something I will always remember, seeing the twins, at seven months old, sitting there in those Devil Ray jerseys and hats. Sydney, just under two years old, also had the time of her life. We sat near the Pirates dugout; I have season tickets near the visiting bench.

The Pirates players were very nice to the kids and my family. Kenny Lofton came over and we talked about basketball. All-Star catcher Jason Kendall and Matt Stairs also came over, and they all took pictures with the family.

Those guys were great to the fans, as they gave a number of baseballs away.

It was a day I will always treasure. Nothing like seeing a child's first day at a ballpark, watching those smiling faces, witnessing the live action, the balls flying, the bats making contact.

My granddaughter also loved Raymond the Mascot, who came over and took a picture. It was total jubilation. It brought joy to a granddad's face for a special day. The smiles were worth the price of admission!

Yes, there was a game and the Devil Rays jumped out 4–0 before the Pirates rallied to get a 9–5 victory.

In time, manager Lou Piniella will turn the Devil Rays around. On this day, the score was secondary. This Father's Day was all about the smiling faces on my grandchildren.

—Reprinted By Permission. Originally appeared on espn.com.

How wonderful it would be if we could help our children and grandchildren to learn thanksgiving at an early age. Thanksgiving opens the doors. It changes a child's personality. A child is resentful, negative—or thankful. Thankful children want to give, they radiate happiness, they draw people.

—SIR JOHN TEMPLETON

We must protect the forests for our children, grandchildren and children yet to be born. We must protect the forests for those who can't speak for themselves such as the birds, animals, fish and trees.

—CHIEF EDWARD MOODY, QWATSINAS,
NUXALK NATION

Joseph Vumbacco

Joseph V. Vumbacco is president and CEO of Health Management Associates, Inc., a Florida corporation that operates acute care hospitals in rural America.

THERE'S A LOT YOU CAN LEARN FROM
YOUR GRANDDAUGHTER

A warm July night in York Beach, Maine, was the perfect time to take Sarah, four, and Sabrina, two, our first grandchildren, to the local beach amusement park. Sarah's an old pro at the park and she crisply articulated exactly which rides the two sisters preferred.

Very little has changed over the thirty-five years our family has enjoyed coastal southern Maine. Both our son and daughter are graduates of the local park's joys, and I suspect Sarah's dad influenced her early in life as to the best and always the final event of the night—the Fun House.

So it was after a solid hour and a half of carrousel, boats, train rides, and the like, that it was time to wrap up with the venerable Fun House with its sagging structure and peeling paint.

"Come on, Poppa," Sarah announced. "You have to take me!"

Of course, there's no turning down that invitation, bad knee notwithstanding. Off we went, up the ladders, through dark halls, gaping at distorted mirrors, until we reached the rotating barrel where the entire family had gathered to cheer our triumphant return. My first instinct was to hold Sarah's hand and lead the way, but when you're a Big Girl of four, no help is needed nor desired. In the wink of an eye, Sarah sped nimbly through the barrel, landing on the opposite side with both feet firmly on the ground.

This is, of course, exactly when I made the big mistake of the evening—overthinking! Sarah's emphatic advice was "Go fast, Poppa," but instead I stepped into the loop and hesitated, if only for a nanosecond, but, as in life, that's all it takes to lose your course. Down I went head over heels with everyone, and I truly mean *everyone*, doubled over with laughter. Somewhere in that brief span of time, a camera was produced, preserving the image for all the years to come.

Finally, emerging from the Fun House with little, if any, dignity remaining, I too had a good belly laugh; but most of all I acknowledged to myself that indeed there are times when old, experienced men should listen to their granddaughters and "just go fast!"

Porter Wagoner

Porter Wagoner is a Grammy Award–winning country music singer and longtime member of the Grand Ole Opry. Known for his one-of-a-kind rhinestone-studded suits, he hosted the Porter Wagoner Show, *one of the most popular country television shows. He was elected to the Country Music Hall of Fame in 2002.*

I love children. I used to be a child myself.

Here's a poem I wrote for my grandchildren:

> *One night when all the stars were lit,*
> *Grandpa went out to stroll a bit.*
> *When he came home Grandma had a fit!*
> *The stars were gone but he was lit.*

Whether they are our own or surrogate grandparents who fill some of the gaps in our mobile society, our senior generation also provides our society a link to our national heritage and traditions.

—PRESIDENT JIMMY CARTER

Mort Walker

Mort Walker is a cartoonist who penned such memorable strips as Hi & Lois *and* Beetle Bailey.

WHEN I'M AROUND MY GRANDCHILDREN I DESCEND TO THEIR LEVEL

MORT WALKER

Mike Wallace

Mike Wallace has been the face of the CBS News program 60 Minutes *since 1968.*

Dear Willard:

In as much as I have eleven of them, and most of them will be with us on the Vineyard during July and August, I shan't have the time or the appetite, I'm sure, to tell you how much fun they are, for the reason that after awhile they can get to be a pain in the a—back!

Good Luck,
Mike Wallace

If you want to know where I come by the passionate commitment I have to bringing people together without regard to race, it all started with my grandfather.

—PRESIDENT BILL CLINTON

Jane and Caspar Weinberger

Jane Weinberger graduated from Boston University with a degree in nursing and used her skills to help the troops during World War II. A published author, she has just retired from running her own publishing company.

Caspar Weinberger served as the United States Secretary of Defense from 1981 to 1987 under President Ronald Reagan. Following public office, he went on to become publisher and chairman of Forbes *magazine. He is the author of* Fighting for Peace: Seven Critical Years in the Pentagon.

*W*e do indeed have grandchildren. Two by the natural process and one acquired when our son married a lady who brought with her a child from a previous marriage—providing us with a very charming little girl. She is now the mother of our two great-grandsons. Our son is the father of our granddaughter and our daughter is the mother of our grandson.

We have had the *pleasure* of providing private schools and colleges, and last year, a wedding reception here in the garden at Windswept when our granddaughter married her longtime friend, now a LT.J.G. in the navy.

They will all be with us for the Christmas holidays, which leads us to mention that the very best thing about grandchildren is that they do go home after a visit.

Willard on the Most Wonderful Things about Being a Grandparent

. . . . . .

Reexperiencing childhood through your grandchildren.

Seeing the joy in your grandchild's eyes when you arrive at the door for a visit.

When you're out and about town with your grandchild, you get to beam with pride when somebody says, "What a beautiful grandchild you have." And you get to beam even more when somebody says, "What a beautiful *child* you have."

Weekends.

Spoiling your grandchildren.

Offering advice to your children—and that advice actually gets accepted.

You share the same interests as your grandchildren—naps, for instance.

. . . . . .

ᕰ·ᕰ·ᕰ

Richard Wilbur

Richard Wilbur is a former poet laureate of the United States and a two-time Pulitzer Prize winner. His numerous books of poetry include New and Collected Poems *and* Things of this World, *which won the National Book Award.*

BLACKBERRIES FOR AMELIA

Fringing the woods, the stone walls, and the lanes,
Old thickets everywhere have come alive,
Their new leaves reaching out in fans of five
From tangles overarched by this year's canes.

They have their flowers, too, it being June,
And here or there in brambled dark-and-light
Are small, five-petaled blooms of chalky white,
As random-clustered and as loosely strewn

As the far stars, of which we now are told
That ever faster do they bolt away,
And that a night may come in which, some say,
We shall have only blackness to behold.

I have no time for any change so great,
But I shall see the August weather spur
Berries to ripen where the flowers were—
Dark berries, savage-sweet and worth the wait—

And there will come the moment to be quick
And save some from the birds, and I shall need
Two pails, old clothes in which to stain and bleed,
And a grandchild to talk with while we pick.

—REPRINTED WITH PERMISSION. FIRST PRINTED IN
THE NEW YORKER, JULY 7, 2003.

Roger Williams

Roger Williams is a nationally renowned pianist who pro-duced thirty-eight hit albums and twenty-two hit singles. His innovative style, combining elements of jazz, pop, and classi-

cal music, as well as his popular appeal, earned him a star on Hollywood's Walk of Fame. He was the first pianist to be so awarded.

I find that one of the most disturbing things about getting old is the fact that whatever subject my grandchildren happen to bring up, I immediately hear myself reciting a lengthy story from my past about that very same subject.

It consistently amazes me that my grandchildren actually listen and seem to enjoy my palaver. Well, bless them!

How I love them all!

Dan Wooding

Dan Wooding is a journalist. He founded the ASSIST News Service, which provides news to 2,600 media outlets around the world. He is also the author of forty-two books and co-hosts a radio show called Window on the World, *in Garden Grove, California.*

Peter, our youngest son, met Sharon, a Welsh girl who was working on a YWAM (Youth With a Mission, a

Christian organization) base in the north of England, shortly after he moved there to work with the group. They fell in love and we went over for their wedding in North Wales. By this time, Peter had been traveling the world and had become the senior news editor for UCB Europe, a Christian radio station in Stoke-on-Trent, England. As the years passed, they presented us with three granddaughters.

Sarah was our first grandchild and was born in 1994, and before she was a year old, she came over to see us with her mother and father, our Peter. We went on a marathon trip through the Californian and Nevada deserts as she sat smiling or sleeping in her baby seat. Anna was next, and as she began to walk, we found that she had a way of not just walking, but running everywhere. She was always on the go. Abigail was the last of the girls, and like the others, loved swimming and didn't seem to have any fear of the water. Most of all, the trio love to entertain. They go to dance classes; Anna goes to ballet and the other two are part of a dance team in their area of North Wales.

Whenever we go and see them, they put on a concert for us as they perform songs and dances that bring such joy. They are such extroverts with great imagination and the two oldest love to write. When we arrive for a visit, they present us with special letters and now they also write to our friends here in Southern California. When we are not there, Peter videos them doing their various musical acts and then sends the tapes over to us, so it is like we are there with them.

After his own YWAM training, our oldest son, Andrew, went into book publishing and worked as an editor for a company in Eastbourne on the south coast of England. He began to write books and has had seven published. He then went to Bradford in Yorkshire, to spend a year attached to an Anglican (Episcopalian) church there before going into training for three years with the Church Army, a branch of the Church of England that does evangelism and social work.

During a visit to England, Andrew sat down with Norma and blurted out that he had "met somebody." He then nervously shared the story of Alison, a Yorkshire lass who was a single mother with two lovely daughters, Jade and Kate. "I am in love with her," he said. "Would you come and meet her?"

Norma went to see Alison in her home and immediately fell in love with her.

When she returned home, she told me the whole story and said that Andrew had invited us to attend his wedding in Bradford. So we flew back across the Pond and watched our older son be joined together with Alison. In 2002, we had a wonderful visit from Andrew, Alison, Jade, and Kate, and enjoyed getting to know the girls better. Jade is a quiet girl who is very beautiful; we were thrilled to take her to swim with the dolphins at Sea World in San Diego, which had been one of her dreams. Kate is a fun-loving girl who recently joined the Girl Guides and is proudly wearing her uniform.

After three years of marriage, they produced Edward Terence, a gurgling, happy, and bonny baby. Our first grandson was born in 2002. He started life a small baby, but he is now growing fast and has a beautiful friendly personality that is evolving, and he seems to lock his blue eyes on everyone who talks to him and gives them a huge smile.

Each time we go to England, we enjoy our singing and dancing granddaughters in North Wales, and then our other grandkids in Sheffield, where Andrew and Alison now live. Norma often sends clothes for them, then our boys take digital pictures of the children with the clothes on and send them to us by e-mail. They also continue to video our grandkids so we can see them growing up.

Even though we are parted physically by thousands of miles, we are bonded together with our extended family in a wonderful way.

Finally Norma and I have realized that if we had not been prepared to give up our two sons and let them go to Britain, we would never have had so much fun with our six grandchildren. They are the joy of our lives!

Afterword

BY WILLARD SCOTT

*W*hat now? We're grandparents, so what are we sup-posed to do?

The answer, short and sweet, is: Be ourselves. Love be-ing with our grandchildren, and love them pure and simple.

The memories you build will not only last a lifetime, but shape your grandchildren's lives—for the better—too. (If you're a mere parent who hasn't achieved grandparent-hood yet, all I can say is that this is something that's better experienced than explained—and when you find out what it's all about, you'll understand how great it all is.)

This is what I have learned from compiling *If I Knew It Was Going to Be This Much Fun, I Would Have Become a Grandparent First*. Working on this book and hearing all these stories about grandparenting has been a privilege, much like the privilege of grandparenting itself. You see, the thing about being a grandparent is that nothing in your life prepares you for how wonderful it is to watch your off-spring a generation removed grow. You see little bits of

user ID:861210011495

user ID:861210011495

title:If I knew It Was Going to
item ID:6012720001959

yourself in them, but you also see things that are brand-new. It's not like looking into a mirror; when you're watching, playing, or just spending time with your grandchildren, it's as if you're looking into a window and seeing a bit of the future.

Your grandchildren look to you, as well, to give them their roots and connections to the past. So you could say that the bond between grandparents and grandchildren is a kind of merging of the past and the future, with bits of the future—our grandchildren—rubbing off on us and keeping us connected to youth with all its hopes and promise, and bits of ourselves—and I hope that's the part with the wisdom—rubbing off on our grandsons and granddaughters. I know that's how it's worked for me and for my family, and I wish the same for you and yours.

Index